MW01103444

A VIEW OF REDEMPTION

MY STORY

A VIEW OF REDEMPTION

MY STORY

Fahren J.

Hunter Heart Publishing
DuPont, Washington

A View of Redemption, My Story

First Edition: October 2010

Please note that the name satan and related names are not capitalized. We choose not to acknowledge him, even to the point of violating grammatical rules.

To order products, or for any other correspondence:

Hunter Heart Publishing
P.O. Box 354
DuPont, Washington 98327
Tel. (253) 906-2160 – Fax: (253) 912-1667
E-mail: publisher@hunterheartpublishing.com
Or reach us on the internet: www.hunterheartpublishing.com

"Offering God's Heart to a Dying World"

This book and all other Hunter Heart Publishing™ books are available at Christian bookstores and distributors worldwide.

Chief Editor: Brenda Mates
Cover Photo by: Latasha Haynes Photography
www. photomelatasha.com
Cover designer: Sigurd Gustafsson
sigurdgustafsson@hotmail.com

ISBN: 978-0-9828377-2-6
For Worldwide Distribution, Printed in the United States of America.

Dedication

Without saying, it has been nothing but God's Grace and the Power of His Holy Spirit that birthed the vision of sharing my testimony. This book is dedicated to the memory of my mom, Helen W. Thomas, and my amazing husband and children: Earnest Lee Johnson III, and my four beautiful children: Myanna Lanise Johnson (17), Ezhane Lashaundra Johnson (16), Earnest Lee Johnson IV (13) and Fianna Gabrielle Johnson (11). I can't imagine where I would be without ya'll. Thank you all for loving me unconditionally.

Fahren J.

Acknowledgements

Without the following people who have stood in the gap with me throughout this life journey, I would not have been able to write this book. Of course my husband, Earnest Johnson, for loving me; it takes a special person to handle this chick, and no one does it like you!

Thank you Virginia Laird, my mother-in-law, who has the greatest patience in the world.

Anna and Rob Groves: who continue to amaze me in their growth as a couple, parents, and in ministry. Anna, thank you for hanging with me for so many years, as my confidant, my home girl, and my best friend. Your friendship means the world to me. I imagine us in our 80's still looking like we are 50, LOL!!

Drs Casey and Wendy Treat and my amazing Christian Faith Center family: What an amazing ministry; the message of renewing the mind has completely changed my life.

Thank you Kim and Marcus Morgan, who have been amazing champions for me in every way.

Thank you Louise Dozier, for just being that voice that speaks truth, even when it hurts.

Thank you Tamika "Mika" Gross, for coming into my life, and bringing such a refreshing friendship!

Thank you Chris and Deborah Hunter for believing in me, and taking on this project; adding your wisdom, expertise, council, and prayers.

Thank you Val and Shaun Alexander, your continued support and prayer over me and my family are truly a God-orchestrated gift. I love you guys!

Sig G, there is just no one greater that I can think of to work with; you are an amazing designer and talent, and an amazing, giving individual. I still remember our deal; if this thing enlarges, I owe you a motorcycle!

Katie Burks, not only my friend and the reason Earnest and I are connected and have a quiver full of children, but now you are my sister in law; how crazy is that!

Arwen and Randy for just sowing so much into my life; you two are the coolest couple.

My sisters of success, Kitty, Clemence, and Junko; how awesome it is to be around women who dream as big as I do!

Latasha and Ike Haynes: Tash, girl your gift, your life, your passion, all of that just blesses me. I'm glad our lives crossed!

Molly V and Jill Cooper, two great women who have entered my life, and in just a short period of time have just blessed me in so many ways!

Ms. Gloria, the pillar, the quiet strength, the intercessor, the woman whose eyes see with the power of the Holy Spirit. Thank you for keeping me focused. I continue to pray that my spirit is so in-tune with the voice of God the way yours is.

My strong and beautiful sister Teresa: who has always, always been there for me and supported me, in the tough times and the good times. I love you Ness; let's get your book done, it will bless so many people!

Jesus, you already know how I feel about You. Thank You for salvation; it is the greatest gift on Earth, and there will never be any way to thank You for all that You have done, but to continue to do the work You have called me to do.

Fahren J.

Foreword

Authenticity.

It's a powerful word. Too bad its presence can be difficult to find in the countless facets of today's media icons, pop culture, and general society. All too often, our leaders and role models from the world around us fall short of the courage it takes to truly be authentic to themselves, to their families, and to their "image."

Fahren J embodies authenticity; in her marriage, with her children, in her music, and most importantly, in her relationship with her Savior. Even the style in which Fahren chooses to write *A View of Redemption, My Story*, her transparency is clearly evident. She writes exactly how she speaks, so that you'll feel, not as though you'd just read an account of her testimony, but rather, as if you'd just sat in the kitchen with her for three hours over a pot of coffee...and maybe more than a few pieces of pie.

It's the same way you feel when you experience Fahren's music. You're not simply listening to excellently crafted and performed music (which it most definitely is), you're engaging with the songwriter herself. You're feeling her journey—warts and all—and how she demanded of herself to never give up, to keep on keepin' on, and to reach beyond her limits with steely faith in her God, until she embraced her victory.

Fahren is a true champion. I have known this amazing woman for almost 10 years, and through this decade, I have seen her choose time and time again, the less-traveled road of authenticity, instead of some other more tempting roads that appeared to be easier, shinier, and trendier. She has chosen her marriage and children over quicker paths to success. She has opted for forgiveness over bitterness, faithfulness over offense, and generosity over apathy. These are tough choices, but the kind of sacrifices authentic champions are willing to make.

A View of Redemption, My Story will inspire you to shake off whatever shackles (big or small) life has tried to bind you with. It will deeply touch your heart, as the love of a Heavenly Father is revealed. And for some of you, these words of Light and Truth will pierce through those dark places you've never dared to expose, and you'll find yourself filled with the courage to take steps toward healing and wholeness.

"You never know one's story, until you've walked in their shoes...walk with me."
~Fahren J
"My Story"
Life Changing Music: Faith, Love, Life

Trust me, this isn't an invitation you want to pass up!

~Molly Venzke

Endorsements

Fahren has emerged from an impossible background to living a life that is full of possibilities. Her whole life is a testimony of God's redemptive grace, as He has walked with her step-by-step from disaster to destiny. Instead of letting circumstances define her, Fahren has become a strong, godly woman who faithfully serves all people with passion and conviction. I believe this book will be a turning point for many hurting people.

~Dr. Wendy Treat, Sr. Pastor,
Christian Faith Center, Federal Way, WA

You would never know just by looking at her, the amazing journey her life has taken. Her smile, her strong spirit of faith, her laughter, her tackle-the-world attitude...Fahren brings life and joy with her wherever she goes, and she just plain "refused to lose!" As I read her story, I could only marvel and say, "Look what the Lord has done!" What He has done for her, He will also do for you!

~Terry Schurman

Reading Fahren's extraordinary account of being born into such horrendous circumstances moved me to tears. As I was led through her story of redemption, I marveled at God's plan, timing, and grace that he lavished on Fahren. What an encouraging story to remind us all of God's love for us!

~Anna Groves

Preface

Defining Moments

Throughout this life journey, we will encounter defining moments that have initiated questions or have answered questions. Throughout this life journey, we hope to discover our earth assignment and the purpose for which we are born. Some of these defining moments have brought joy, and some have evoked pain. Some defining moments have caused insanity, and some have created success. Some defining moments cause weakness; some conjured strength. When it comes down to it, as long as we have breath in our bodies, we will be in process of definition.

The question is, who and what will we allow to define us? Is it the job, the friends, the mom or dad, the past, your present, the husband or wife, your children, a teacher, physical or sexual abuse, the future, the one and true God, your gifts or talents, your abundance or lack, what you wear or what color you are? Defining moments can bring restoration; all it takes is faith to reach for God's Lifeline to change destiny.

Table of Contents

Chapter 1

She Child
~She comes because purpose called her name~

Ecclesiastes 3:1 (KJV)
*"To every thing there is a season, and a time to every purpose
under the heaven."*

A young woman, hair standing wildly on her head, is screaming and moaning, while being wheeled through a hospital lobby.
She is obviously in labor. Once in the delivery room, she is
placed on a gurney bed. In walks the doctor; he walks over to the
sink, scrubs, and puts on his sanitized gloves and surgical mask.
He walks over to the delivery bed, looks at the woman, and
shakes his head wondering who would impregnate an obviously
mentally ill woman. The woman can sense his judgment, and
escapes into the safety of her mental darkness; she screams and
pushes, and pushes and pushes some more. The sound of a baby

crying echoes the delivery room. "It's a girl," the doctor announces mechanically. This woman is swimming wildly in her thoughts to find a moment of reality. It comes and goes, and she is always aware that the moments of reality do not last very long. The moment comes, and she eagerly waits for the nurse to place her baby girl into her arms. The moment passes; no baby. She fights through her darkness again, and dares to hope that her baby will be in her arms, but the moment passes again. The doctor snips the baby's umbilical cord, turns, and hands the now quiet baby to the nurse. The nurse cleans and wraps the baby girl, and turns walking through the double doors, out of the delivery room; baby in her arms.

The young woman sits up in her bed and begins to kick and scream wildly, "My baby, give me my baby, do not take my baby, please do not take my baby", she calls after the nurse, "Her name is Fahren, her name is Fahren", she screams between sorrowful sobs and wails… "Did you hear me?" The nurse locks eyes with the woman, whispers something into the baby's ear, and they disappear down the hallway. The woman is hysterical, and becomes more and more uncontrollable. She feels a poke, and is now getting very sleepy. Finally, she closes her eyes, and escapes into the safety of her darkness. "Her name is Fahren", she whispers sleepily, and the room fades to darkness. When she wakes up, her legs and arms are strapped to the bed; someone is pushing her down a hallway and into a door with the sign "Mental Patient Ward" on the front of it.

My name is Fahren; the name the nurse whispered into my ear, as my mom watched her walk out of the delivery room. I am so glad that God knew my name before I was born. I am glad He knew me, before I was born. Little did I know that from birth, God was redeeming and re-defining me, and continues to do so to this day. My birth mother, Francine, suffers from Paranoid Schizophrenia. During her stay in a mental hospital, she conceived a child. That child was me. To this day, I have no clue to who my father is. I am told that my mother was taken advantage of while she was in a mental institution. Taken from her at about 6 months of age, I became a Ward of the State and placed in the foster care system.

Many would say that my life was doomed from the beginning. I do not have a relationship with my birth mother, and I have no clue to who my father is. The woman I am today gives no reflection of a life of doom. However, the emotional and spiritual journey I had to take to get to this place in my life was not easy, and will always be a work in progress, until I leave this earth. Life is choice, and choice is Key. I know that tomorrow is not promised, and each morning when I open my eyes, I am thankful that God's plan and purpose has awakened me.

Father God,

I pray now for the one who is holding and preparing to read this book. I pray that they realize this is a divine appointment. That it not just sit meaningless on a shelf or in the palm of their hands. I thank You that they have sown into something that will be a blessing to them, spiritually and emotionally. Let the power of Your Holy Spirit bring life and revelation. Let it lift and encourage, build and reinforce, uproot and replant, nourish and refresh, and remind them of this very special promise from You God, which is this: they matter. They are loved. You know the plans You have for them, no matter what situation, decision, sickness, or natural disaster that has come their way. I thank You right now that these words will touch and reach into the hidden parts of their heart and minister in a way that only Your Word can do. Let the power of testimony set them free and send them straight into Your wonderful Love and Salvation.

In Jesus' mighty name,

Amen

Chapter 2

Belonging

~What is it you're searching for? You stop and then you go?
Looking for something more?~

Proverbs 20:2 (NKJV)
"The spirit of a man is the lamp of the LORD,
Searching all the inner depths of his heart."

I entered into the foster care system at six months of age. The first four years of my life are memories I will never know, locked away in an old case file; sealed away in an archive somewhere. I do remember from the ages of five and on that I was a quiet little girl; observant and extremely introspective. I never really liked to be unsure of anything. I didn't like puzzles, riddles, or anything that required me to guess or figure out, or be left to assume. I didn't like uncertainty. I did not do well with change, or unexpected interruptions. It was important for me to always know what was going on; where I was going, why I was going, how long was I going to be there, and when was I going to arrive. If I was unsure of something, I didn't engage. I became a pro at detaching, so to the point that I carried this negative behavior into the other areas of my life. If someone said something that was hurtful, mean, or sarcastic, I could literally mute that person instantly. I would see their mouth moving, but hear nothing.

I didn't understand at the time, but I realized later that it was my defense mechanism. I was a foster child, I moved to several homes, until the state found a stable home that had the potential of being my permanent residence. I innately regulated my emotions; keeping all things strictly surface to what I could see or what I could touch. Those who know me now see me as a strong Faith woman. However, as a young child, I guess you could say I was not the best candidate to live by Faith. I operated in the opposite of Faith; I maneuvered within fear. In my eyes, it was easier to never totally trust or connect to anything, as if I was always prepared for the "just in case, it doesn't work out." I know now that, sadly, I had no sense of belonging.

I was around six years old, when I began to have this vivid and bothersome dream, but I did not muster up the nerve to share the dream until I was about eight years old. I remember sitting on my bed talking to my sister, and I began to tell her about this dream. The vision would give me the viewer perspective, as if I were watching scenes unfold; never physically participating in it. Yet, somehow, I always felt connected to what was happening. The images would flash across my eyes like an old school, black and white picture show. It would start with a ladder extending up to a window; the image would pan back to reveal a fire engine parked on the side of the street. I would then see a woman clutching two small children. She was screaming horribly as if someone was violating her in the worst way. I would then see two fire-fighters enter through the window, and one holding what looked like a long, metal crowbar in his hand, and then just as quickly as it came, the vision would stop.

My sister listened as I described the series of events and the images that I had been seeing. She paused and responded…"We were on a supervised visit to see our birth mom. The social worker came to pick us up that day, and drove us to Grandma's house. You were 4 years old and I was almost 7 years old. I remember mom was very distracted that day. Grandma has an attic upstairs in her room, and I remember mom taking us up to the attic."

"For a while, we just sat and she played with us, but after a few moments, she began to cry. I remember Grandma coming to the attic door, and trying to open it, but mom had locked the door. She kept calling to her, 'Open the door, it's time for the girls to go back.' I remember "mom" kept saying, 'No I am keeping them with me, and no one is taking my babies away from me again.' Grandma did not want to upset her too much, so she tried to persuade her to open the door. She promised her all sorts of things, but mom was not buying it. She was determined that no one was going to take us from her again. Grandma ended up having to call the police to come and break into the attic. It was quite the scene. Everyone in the neighborhood watched the whole thing unfold. I remember looking out of the window and all of the neighbors, the social worker, the police, and firefighters were outside on the front lawn."

"They sent a fire engine truck, so that they could extend the ladder to the attic window and pull us out." My sister continued, "Mom was holding you and ran to the window and pulled me back from it. She was squeezing us in her arms so tight, I thought I was going to suffocate. She kept screaming 'No, no, leave us alone, these are my babies, my babies.' The firefighter broke the attic window and came in to the attic room followed by another firefighter. Mom fought them off, like a momma bear defending her cubs to the death. They were trying not to hurt us, attempting to pull her arms open, but they could not. The more they pulled on her, the more hysterical and stronger she became, and I thought we were going to die from being crushed in her arms.

The firefighters had a crowbar; one got behind her, and the other stuck the crowbar in between her and us and began to pry us out of her arms. I will never forget the scream; it was as if she knew that this would be the last time she would ever see her babies again. After finally wearing her down, until she had no strength left to fight, she surrendered us to the firefighters and they quickly grabbed us and backed out the window and down the ladder. We never saw mom or grandma again."

When my sister finished describing what seemed like some-thing out of movie, I remember having a hard time processing it. This was my first time hearing about a woman I did not remem-ber, except only in a dream, and to add to it, this woman is supposedly my mother? No, I thought, my sister is mistaken. Just like I know she is my sister, because she has always been in the same home with me, I thought I knew who I belonged to? My mother's name was Helen W. Thomas. She is the only woman I have ever called mom. She has always been the one who took care of me, loved me, and invited me into all of her environment. She always had children around; some would come, some would go, and I never really thought much of it, because I was never one of the children that would "go". I assumed I belonged to her. She never told me that I didn't belong to her. How ironic, the same day I decided to share my dream with my sister, the woman I've always known to be my mother comes home that day, announcing that she is now our legal mother, and that our adoption was final.

What is belonging? Webster's Dictionary defines the word "belonging" as: Possession; an intimate or close relationship to someone or something. I feel that belonging is another word for Identity. I firmly believe that inside of us all is a compass, which God wove into the physical and spiritual DNA of our being, and it is always trying to point us back to Him, our Creator, to whom we belong.

Psalm 139: 16 (MSG)
"Like an open book, you watched me grow from conception to birth; all the stages of my life were spread out before you, the days of my life all prepared before I'd even lived one day".

I love the way the Message Bible magnifies this verse in Psalm, because David paints a clear picture of the created realizing just how much it's connected to its Creator.

Today, you need to know that the days of your life were planned before your father's sperm joined your mother's egg; before your cells began to multiply and form the intricate detailing of the human body; before breath was yours, God had it with Him an eternity ago. No matter what situation you are going through right now, no matter what you may have gone through, if you get a hold of this one thing, that you belong to God, the process of searching no longer will be like chasing wind, or trying to touch a shadow that you will never feel. You have been identified in the flesh, but more importantly, in the Spirit.

I have searched, and tried every avenue to answer that question of "Who am I?" I tried to settle it in my abilities, thinking that if I worked hard enough that my works would define me. I tried to settle it in relationships by being a people-pleaser, thinking that if I could gain the attention of people that would define me. I tried to settle it with re-connecting with my birth family, thinking if I could only fill in the missing pieces, I would be whole. None of these things filled that void. It may have seemed satisfying for a moment, but after a while, that compass would begin turning, and I would start my search all over again.

I am no longer in the place of searching, but it is only because I realized I've been trying to belong to the wrong thing. I've been looking at the created to fill something that only my Inventor, Creator, my God could fill. I allowed my ability to detach me from not just the emotional and physical being, but my spiritual being as well. The very thing I was trying to protect myself from was blocking me from receiving what I was looking for. I believe that everyone will experience moments in life where revelation finally becomes real. It happens at different stages of life. I wish some revelations would have come sooner than others, but I understand also that some come during the walking out of living life. Some lessons have to be lived, in order to be learned. If my walking it out can help someone take a step in the direction of freedom, sooner than later, then it was not in vain.

In God, through Christ, I have found my identity, and His Spirit has been the compass that I sensed the entire time, but never connected to. If that is you, it's time for you to get connected to your compass. To do that, you must first connect to your one and only Creator, God. To get to Him, there is only one way, through Jesus Christ. We will re-visit this a little later on, but I want to allow this truth to sit and marinate a little more. In the meantime, come... take a walk with me.

Chapter 3

Fostering My Roots
~From the start of Eternity, He spoke my name~

Jeremiah 1:5a (NKJV)
"Before I formed you in the womb I knew you..."

If you are a foster parent, I want to say thank you for giving yourself unselfishly to ensure that the child or children you have taken into your home are loved and positioned in a direction that they otherwise would have never had. I think that it takes a very special person to open their home up to children who are going through difficult situations. Not everyone has the desire or compassion to raise someone else's child. Even more so, being a transitional home and never knowing how long you will have the child. It takes strength and faith, and a knowing that no matter how long you foster a child, whether it is for one week or one year, you understand that your purpose is to give that child as much love and support as you possibly can, in hopes that you help to change the direction of their future.

I became a foster-adopted child, legally at the age of 8 years old. My adoptive parents were James Henry and Helen Windom Thomas. My adoptive dad was one of 13 children from Vicksburg, Mississippi, and my adoptive mother was the oldest of 14 children from Cecil, Georgia.

They were an older couple in their late 50's when I came into the home. They met by way of Chicago; my mom was writing for a newspaper column and my father was passing through on his way to Alaska, where he was working on the pipeline. My mom had been married before, to a musician who was completely eaten up by his dependence on drugs; she had been divorced for quite some time. When she met my dad, he swept her off of her feet; they dated and he convinced her to move to Anchorage with him. There, they were married. They lived in Fairbanks for 10 years, and Anchorage another 10 years. My adoptive mom was unable to have children, because at a young age, they discovered cysts on her ovaries and uterus. Unequal health care and being black during that time, robbed her from being able to afford medical care, and instead of the doctors finding a treatment, the doctors just gave her a complete hysterectomy.

They adopted their first son, my adopted brother Reggie, while they were in Alaska. When my dad retired from the pipeline, he was offered an opportunity to work in the Pacific Northwest, and was connected to an asphalt company in Washington State. They decided to relocate to Tacoma, WA. My dad had a fifth grade education, and never finished school. He could not read, and committed everything to memory. He always worked and found good paying jobs, despite his minimal education. He was the funniest man, likeable, and made friends with anyone that he met; no one was a stranger.

My adoptive mom, as a young girl, went to school in a one-room school house. Despite the heavy segregation and racism she encountered along the way, she fought to earn her degree in child psychology and also an undergrad degree in journalism. She found a job working with community focused programs that fostered children and youth well-being. She was an extremely driven and community focused individual. She was well liked in the Tacoma community and spearheaded a lot of community programs for seniors, homeless, and youth. She was a 4-H leader, an active member of her church, a member of local clubs in her community, and a community project coordinator. Anyone who came into her home was partnering in some way with her in community work, or strategizing on a project. I can honestly say that she excelled in her gift of serving.

I believe that there are some gifts that are passed on generationally, and there are some personality styles you take on when you spend time with someone for many years. I can definitely say that I appreciate being raised by a woman who believed in serving her community. It is part of the foundation of who I am, I love to serve. In being a server, there are pros and cons, and I learned later in life how important it is that a server must learn how to balance this gifting and passion, or it will cause havoc later in life.

My adoptive mom made sure we went to Sunday school and Vacation Bible School during the summer. I truly appreciate the foundation she laid for all of her foster children, to at least get us to a place where we could learn that there is someone who is greater. She had even organized her church to drive their buses through apartment complexes every Sunday morning to pick up children that wanted to go to vacation summer school. As I look back, I realized that we didn't pray at home, or read, or discuss the Bible. So, I learned how to go to church, learned the basics of who Jesus was, and like most children, I was afraid of going to hell, so I did my best not to disobey my parents, and to treat people the way I wanted to be treated. I never established my own personal relationship with Christ, nor decided to fully accept Him as my Lord and Savior, until I was in my twenties.

I don't think I ever remember my adoptive dad going to church, except one time in my entire life, but he was not a bad person. He had a different way of serving people by making them laugh, and helping them to find work. He didn't like to be around a lot of people, but knew everyone in town, because he had such a one on one, people personality. His only true commitment to all of the foster children was that he worked hard to make sure my mom had the things she needed to care for us. Other than that, we looked to our adoptive mom for everything.

My adoptive mom found out that I had a half sister, who was also a Ward of the State. She researched until she found her and brought her to her home, so that we would be raised together. Her name is Teresa, and she is a couple of years older than I. We have been raised together from the time we were four and seven years old. As I think about it, my adoptive mom did that with almost all of the children she fostered. She would request that if a child had siblings, that they all be placed with her and not be separated. I am so thankful for her heart to see families stay together; she had to really fight for this, but managed to succeed in most of the children she fostered.

Her foster home consisted of elementary and high school teens that suffered themselves from various forms of abuse. She had a diverse group of children, all ages and all colors. I know her heart was in the right place, and her passion was to create a safe place for young kids to grow. I feel; however, that the state's objective was to hurry up and find a place for a child to go, no matter what. I don't think that she thought through how the differing of ages and mixing them in a home together would play out; it was admirable, but not the best option. Her passion to be available to all foster children consequently meant that the state would send her youth that had challenges being placed in homes.

Unfortunately, she was not adequately informed of issues that some of the foster kids faced in their birth home, or recent foster care home. Children are destined to repeat what happens to them, if they are not renewed or shown how to think and act differently. Child abuse, whether physical or sexual, was a huge challenge in the foster care system. My adoptive mom's home seemed to be the home where alot of children who suffered from these abuses were placed. I, and my sister Teresa, suffered because of it.

Chapter 4

Fear Steals
~ I've been through some things that caused me pain, but I refuse to lose~

Philippians 4:13
"I can do all things through Christ who strengthens me."

From the ages of 9 years old until about 12 years old, my sister and I became victims of molestation by the teen foster boys that came into the home and by family friends; it was horrible. Our bodies did not belong to us; they belonged to whoever felt attracted to it. As a parent of three teenagers and a "tweenie", I can't imagine someone violating them in any way, shape, or form. The mentality of a nine year old, as well as their perception of love, is still developing. Add sexual abuse to the equation, and their view of sex, which is supposed to be beautiful, becomes twisted, as well as the definition of love.

I remember the night visits my sister and I would get. We would hear the door creek open, and just pray that the abuser would not get into our bed that night. I carried this weight of guilt for many years that for some reason, I brought this on myself. I would try to make myself small, un-noticeable, and plain, as to not attract any attention. I was ruled by self-blame, and it kept me from seeking out help. The detachment I spoke about earlier was my best defense. Whenever the abuse would happen, I would literally be able to imagine myself somewhere else, and I would just go there. I learned how to numb my pain. Completely un-plugged from what was really happening, my abusers became faceless. It was my coping mechanism; if I didn't see the face, I could separate abuser from brother, abuser from aunt or uncle, and abuser from trusted friends of the family.

By the age of 12, I was fed up with not having control over my body. I remember the day I decided to tell my mom what had been happening to my sister and me. I told her everything, and her response was the total opposite of what I expected. Not only did she not believe us, but we were punished for even making what she thought were horrible accusations. I was so disap-pointed. My sister eventually left the home, and I could see that her respect for my adopted mom was diminishing, and eventually was the wedge that severed their relationship. I didn't have the guts to just leave, but I refused to keep living and hiding such a horrible situation. I decided that if my mom went anywhere, she was going to take me with her, point blank. When she would leave, I would act so horribly that no one would want to keep me, not even my adopted dad. No one realized that this is how I was saving myself.

My adoptive mom took me everywhere with her, not because she wanted to, but because she had to. I could have grown into a very withdrawn, bitter person, and at times, it felt like I had every right to be. My choice to press instead of regress was supernatural. Even though I felt powerless, I knew that there was someone watching over me, because I was still here, still standing.

If I was not at school, or participating in some sort of extra-curricular activity, I went to work with her, I went to school with her; I was attached to her hip at all times. We exhibited clear signs that something was going on, but no one discerned or paid very much attention. Eventually, the abuse stopped, partly because the abusers transitioned out of the home, and because I was never around. It was never spoken of and never dealt with; it was as if it never happened, but the affects of sexual abuse manifested and re-surfaced in my life as a young adult.

Despite the challenges, I refused to lose. Even in the midst of that very dark time in my life, I excelled in my teen years. High school was rather freeing for me, so I did exactly what my adopted mom did. I took every negative thing that happened to me during my adolescent years, and pushed it down as far as I could. Since I didn't know how to really communicate how I was feeling, I just poured myself into doing things that I was good at. I was an athlete and a gymnast for 10 years. I played Varsity volleyball and ran track. I stayed busy and active in school, made a lot of acquaintances, and built cool relationships, but I was not a cliquish person; I never allowed myself to get tied to too many relationships for too long. I developed this strong dislike for bullies, and to people who took advantage of those they consi-dered weak. I was the one who rooted for the underdog. The thought of someone being used or mistreated for any reason just bugged me with a passion.

I learned to be a people reader, and I observed everything; even when people had no idea that I was watching. I always wanted to know what the true intentions of people were. I was a great athlete, and it came with cool perks, but if I felt like someone was trying to connect to me specifically because of my ability or notoriety, I quickly backed away. I was carefully discerning who I would allow into my confidant circle. I truly was not, and still to this day am not, interested in superficial relationships.

When I was in high school, I promised myself that I would never let another person take advantage of me. I was going to always be in control of my destiny. That attitude turned out to be a horrible way of looking at things, but at the time, you could not tell me there was any other way. My adoptive mom finally retired from being a foster mother, but she always opened her home up to anyone who was in need. By the time I was a junior, I had taken on a nanny job, and moved in with the family I worked for, so I was very rarely home anymore. I was a nanny for a Caucasian couple who had 3 beautiful children; 2 boys and a girl. I loved them like they were my siblings; I enjoyed watching them grow up, and I enjoyed the feeling of independence.

I was a strong writer; I remember writing my first song when I was 8 years old. I really took to writing in high school, and it became the voice behind my voice. I was amazed at how I could communicate exactly how I felt on paper. I also loved to sing, and it just went together so perfectly. I was not an orator, but if you gave me a pen and a microphone, I could sing about it better than I could talk about it.

These were hidden gifts that I just viewed as hobbies. It was not until much later in life that I would even consider trying to do more with it. Eventually, track and field became the sport that really set me on a pathway of what looked like a great future. I guess you could say, from the outside looking in, and to many people, I was a champion. I was an All-State Champion for 3 years in high school Track and Field. I was named Tacoma Athlete of the Year my Senior Year. I went to Nationals in California and placed second in the nation against athletes from all over the US in Triple Jump, and went on to London, England that summer and competed against top high school athletes from around the world, and brought home the Championship in the Triple Jump event. I was recruited heavily by Universities from all over; Stanford, Notre Dame, University of Oregon, Washington State, even West Point's athletic department, just to name a few. I still have all of my recruiter letters and trophies in a chest, and I pull them out from time to time. I accepted a full ride scholarship offer to the University of Washington, and it looked like I was moving closer to my dreams and goals of accomplishing more than what my parents had accomplished. It appeared that anything I set my hand to prospered.

I remember when I would go to church we would read about Moses and Joseph, great men of God, and the children of Israel, the chosen people of God. I was more at that time a literal reader, and was never really taught, or interested, in digging deeper into God's Word for revelation. I used to ask so many questions like, "Why did it take so long for these "Great people, called of God" to tap into all God had for them. How come Moses had to flee from his home and become a foreigner for 40 years, before he became a leader? Why was Joseph betrayed by his own brothers and sold into slavery, before he became a leader. Why did the children of Israel, God's people whom He rescued, have to wander for so many years, and the journey was only supposed to be 3 days?" I remember thinking to myself and then talking to God, "Lord, I just don't have that kind of patience. I am too driven, so you are going to have to help me work this area out." I asked this in all sincerity of my heart. Boy, did I learn to be ever so careful about what you ask for, especially if it is necessary for God to accomplish His plan and will for your life.

The summer break between graduating and starting my freshman year at the University of Washington was the start of an interesting emotional time for me. From the time that my adoption was final, I was not allowed to visit or inquire about my birth family. The only reason I knew that my birth family even lived in the same city was due to my sister leaving our adoptive home, going to a group home, and then eventually tracking down information about our birth family. She actually went to live with my birth grandmother for a year. When I graduated, this was the first thing on my list to do. I got in contact with my sister, and she helped to coordinate my first visit with my birth grandmother and mother.

I remember having to fight this feeling of betrayal. I was so attached to my adoptive mom that I did not tell her what I was planning, because I did not want her to think that I was abandoning her or didn't love her. In my mind, she was my mom, she didn't birth me, but she was my mother; I knew nothing or no one could ever change my heart about this. I did; however, know that this was a tender spot for her, so this was my way of caring for her feelings. I remember talking to my sister, and her telling me that there was a possibility that we had other siblings, and just the idea of having other siblings was exciting.

I remember the day like it was yesterday. My sister came and picked me up, and we headed over to my grandmother's house. When we pulled up, I almost choked; it was the same house in my dreams, and that horrible attic window. Fear just overtook me. It was overwhelming; I've never felt anything like it before. This whole time, I lived in the same city as my birth mother and grandmother, on the exact opposite side of town. My sister got out of the car and popped her head back into the window. Are you coming? The longest walk of my life was the walk from my sister's car to the front door of my grandmother's house.

She opened the door, and it was as if time had never separated us. My grandmother welcomed me with open arms, saying "Hello precious", hugged me long and snug, stepped back and proclaimed, "You look just like your mother." When I walked in, another older woman was sitting in the living room. My sister introduced her and she said, "Fahren, this is Luanna, this is our oldest sister." I remember looking at her and saying, "Wow, you and Teresa look just alike", and then I looked at my grandmother again, and thought, oh my goodness, you two look just like Grandma! So, I found out all in one day that not only did I have one sister, but I had 3 sisters and 1 brother, and we all were birthed from the same womb. The meeting of all of my birth family will continue in another book, so stay tuned!

Naomi Cooper, my grandmother, stood about 5ft. 8 inches tall, full-figured, and about 60 years old when I met her for the first time. Her home was huge, about 5 bedrooms, and located in a beautiful neighborhood near the waterfront. I could tell off of the bat that she was a spiritual woman. She had this sweet joy and peace about her, and being in her company was just easy. She just hugged me and hugged me, and said, "I have been waiting for you." I had so many questions; I had to force myself to sit and take all of this in. I'm sure she could sense the wrestle I was having internally, and before I could open my mouth to ask my series of soul searching questions, she turned her head and called over her shoulder, "Franny, you have visitors, come on up and say hello." I was taken from my mother too young to remember what she looked like. Even in my re-occurring dream, I never saw her face. It was always a blur.

I was never told that she suffered from a mental illness, not even my sister mentioned it. I was just told that she was not well. So, at this very moment, I was about to meet my birth mother for the first time. I could hear footsteps coming up the stairs, and not too long after that a small framed woman came from the hallway holding a coffee cup in one hand and a cigarette in the other. It was the middle of summer, and she had a beanie cap on her head, while wearing a sweat suit. Her head was hung, as she walked swiftly by us and headed to the kitchen. I was trying to look at her face, but she wouldn't look up or slow down. When she passed by me, I had an overwhelming sense of sadness, and I cried. My sister's were silent. They never said a word. I felt like they knew so much more than me, and I was kept in the dark this entire time.

My grandmother called out to her, "Franny, do you know who you just passed?", and she answered back from the kitchen, "Yes, that's Fahren." First of all, I was amazed at her voice; it was so unique and beautiful, almost like she was probably a great singer before she started smoking. Secondly, this woman had not seen me since I was around four years old, barely looked at me, and she positively knew who I was. I had to see her face, I just had too. I looked back towards the kitchen, and this woman was staring at me. It was the most uncomfortable feeling ever. I quickly tried to scan her to see if I actually looked like her. I had her lips, I had her eyes, I had her body build, and I had her nose. It was strange connecting to someone you should know, but have never known. When I turned away from her, I could feel her staring at me. Just as quickly as she emerged, she was gone, passing by me and back downstairs.

My grandmother interrupted the odd silence, and responded "You have to give her some time, she didn't only lose you, but all of her children were taken from her at a young age. Having all three of you girls here at one time is just too much for her. She has shut down. Time has stopped for her; she never moved passed the moment you were taken from her, so she does not know how to merge her past and present." I couldn't hold it any longer; I had to ask this one question, if nothing else. I said "Grandma, why is she not well?" My reasoning in asking this question was that most of the foster kids that came into our home were taken from their mothers due to sexual abuse, or drug use that resulted in the neglect or harm of the child. So, I just assumed she was not well from maybe being on drugs.

My grandmother answered my question. "She has suffered from schizophrenia from the time she was 28 years old, which means that she sees and hears things that are not really there. Prior to her breakdown, she was married with 3 children; her relationship with her husband was very toxic. When he left her, he took your three older siblings from her and left her in a mental institution in another state. I had to go get her and bring her to the Pacific Northwest. She was early in pregnancy with your sister at the time. I had to admit her into the mental institution here in Washington for several months to get her stable, before she was well enough for me to be able to care for her."

As my grandmother was talking, my mind was calculating and processing her words. I began to think, "Well, if all of my other siblings have the same father, clearly, I don't. So who is my father?" I didn't find out until much later about the circumstances surrounding my conception. Grandma continued, "When you were taken from her, she was already very fragile in her illness; you were the second set of children that were physically taken from her again. It was the last traumatic experience that broke her, and she has been this way ever since. She stays downstairs in a dark room; she is very uncomfortable around people, and isolates herself 90% of the time. Some days are better than others. She has times of reality, but it's very few; she lives in the past where her sanity ceased to exist, and is consumed by voices and people whom she talks to all night long. She has been in and out of a mental institution for many years."

I was sick to my stomach; I had heard that word schizophrenia before, in my high school psychology class, and my instructor defined it as: a severe mental disorder characterized by some, but not necessarily all of the following features: emotional blunting, intellectual deterioration, social isolation, disorganized speech and behavior, delusions, and hallucinations. It usually is a mental illness that is inherited or transferred generationally. The only thing I could hear burning in my ears was the last phrase of that definition- a mental illness that is inherited or transferred generationally.

I was ready to go; I should not have come here, I thought to myself. I looked at my sister and she already knew that I was done. I got up, I hugged my grandma, and the last thing she said to me was, "I have always prayed for you. I can't tell you why this happened, and I won't be able to give you all of the answers to your questions, but God knows; ask the Holy Spirit to speak to you." I remember saying to my grandmother, while she embraced me, "Grandma, I don't even know what a Holy Spirit is." She replied, "Well precious, I suggest it's time you have a little talk with Jesus." From that day, three years would go by before I would go back to my grandmother's house again.

Chapter 5

Life is Choice, Choice is Key
~to lay it all down, I'm ready~

John 13:38a (NKJV)
"Jesus answered him, "Will you lay down your life for My sake?"

That encounter the summer of 1991 changed something in me. I remember having these odd episodes where out of the clear blue, my heart would start racing, and I would literally feel like I was dying. I would never tell anyone about them; I never mentioned it to my doctor. I figured if I ignored it, it would just go away. I determined that when I got to college, I would never tell anyone about being adopted, or the fact that I was born to a mentally ill mother. I kept it all hidden, partly because I was very ashamed and I didn't want anyone to judge me because of my background. I was so hard on myself; I would say, "Wow Fahren, you used to get so mad at your mom for keeping secrets, and look at you; you are following right in her footsteps." I did my best to sever any relationships I had from high school. I was starting a new life, and I vowed that I was never going back to my hometown once I left. The odd episodes, I just kept to myself.

I will never forget when my mom and dad drove me up to the University of Washington campus. My dorms were called Terry/Lander. My roommate was this real cool chick from LA. I was like yes, I am grown now; I am in control. My track coach was this cool Puerto Rican cat, and I was just excited to be a part of a PAC-10 university athletic team. I just blazed through my freshman year; academically and athletically. I placed 7th in the Pac-10 Track championships in the Triple Jump, and was named University of Washington's most valuable freshman of the year. I started dating towards the end of my freshman year, after a pretty hard break up with a guy who I met when I was in high school, and re-entered my life when I got to college. He was at Notre Dame on a football scholarship, and had to come home for a semester. I remember coming in from track practice, and he was sitting there in the lobby waiting for me. I was pretty sure that I was going to marry this guy, and just like he appeared in my dorm lobby, one day, he just disappeared. No explanation, no phone call; nothing.

My feelings were so hurt; I vowed that day that I would never give my heart to a man, because all they did was just take and never gave me what I needed. The pattern of keeping people at arm's length was just automatic. I didn't know how, nor did I want to let anyone completely in. It was definitely an unhealthy behavior, but I did not know how to operate any other way. I would hang out, but I was never a big drinker and I didn't smoke; none of that, because I believed in keeping my body conditioned to perform and win.

I loved to dance. I remember the day I met this girl that would ultimately be a great friend and the key to my life taking another major transition. It was a Wednesday night at the club, and I was dancing. She walks up to me, and the music is loud, but she is looking at me, like she is about to talk smack. Now, I didn't just let people talk crazy to me, or even look like they wanted to, so I walked over said, "What's up, why are you looking at me?" She says, "You are in my spot", and I say, "And, what's the problem?" She says, "You need to move." I'm like, "Move me"...so we are definitely getting ready to get it done up in this club, and my girls and her girls jump in between us. I was thinking whatever, and went right back to the same spot I was dancing in, wishing she would come find me.

So the next morning, I am on my way to the shower, and guess who comes around the corner on their way to shower. The same girl I was getting ready to fight at the club. We paused, looked at each other, and just started cracking up laughing. From that day on, we were inseparable. We had so much in common. We encountered some of the same challenges in our life. She was a foster child that was later adopted. It was just crazy. Her name was Katie Burks, and meeting her changed the direction of my life forever.

Throughout my freshman year, I still hid my episodes of feeling like I was dying; I just could not figure out why I would have this feeling. I told Katie everything about me, except for that one thing. Every time I would have one, I would think, "Uh oh, this is it; I'm turning into a schizophrenic." I was just sure that eventually, I was going to end up like my birth mother. I was not in a committed relationship, because I was still healing from the shattered heart earlier that school year. Katie was a year ahead of me in school; we spent most of our time hanging out in her room.

I used to tease her, because the guy she was dating only came around at night, and I barely ever saw him. I used to call him the "boyfriend ghost". Yet, his brother and his friends used to hang out with her all of the time. I was like dang, which one of these guys is the real boyfriend. I still was not interested in any relationships, so I was not aware of anyone wanting to hook up with me. Katie used to tell me, "Fahren, my boyfriend's brother thinks you are so beautiful." And I would always reply, "Really, oh...I'm not interested."

One night we needed a ride home from the club, and it just happened that Katie's boyfriend's brother was there and he had a car. She said, "Let's ask him for a ride home", and I'm like, "No thank you", and she said, "Why not, he is really nice?" I replied, "Let's just catch the bus." Katie says, "Fahren, he is really nice, you will like his personality." Finally I say yes, not realizing this entire time, that this was part of Katie's and his plan to try and hook up with me. We get to his car, and Katie gets to the car before me, and hops in the back seat. Smiling at me, she says, "You sit in the front." If looks could have killed that night, Katie would have died from the glare I gave her. Turns out, he was the coolest dude I had ever met; very level headed, respectful, and absolutely hilarious, and he was originally from the south.

We hung out a lot that summer, mainly in group settings; me and my girls, and he and his boys. He was not bad looking either; I still wasn't trying to have a serious relationship, but we eventually went out on our first official date. We talked until the sun came up. I will never forget that night, because he told me straight out, "You are going to be my wife." I was like, okay, sure, I don't know about that. I was 18 turning 19 when I started going steady with Earnest Lee Johnson III, the absolute love of my life.

So, my sophomore year I didn't have to stay on campus. Katie and I decided to get an apartment together; my scholarship allowed a certain amount of money towards rent. The only problem we had was that we didn't have any credit. So I asked my boyfriend, Earnest, if he would co-sign for an apartment with us, and we would all be roommates. We loved our apartment; my adoptive mom gave me some furniture, and then we rented some of the other stuff. We didn't have a car, but I didn't live too far from school, and just commuted to class and practice via the bus.

The indoor track season was starting, and we had begun our training in August. I was close with another teammate; her name was Koko, and she was the coolest chick. I remember it was mid-September, and we were at Heck–Ed stadium getting ready to run some drills. I was stretching, and one of my guy friends, who played football at the U, poked me in my side and was like, "Wow Fahren, you have gotten thick." My girlfriend Koko looked at me, and I looked at her, and was like what is he talking about, do I look fat? She was like, "No not at all; you look like you are in great shape to me." I have never had a normal period, so if I missed a cycle, I didn't stress about it. I was with Earnest, and I always used protection, so I really didn't think much of it.

A month goes by, and I am warming up for my first indoor race of the season, the 50 meter hurdles. I had eaten a little something for breakfast, and was still feeling really full. It seemed like I had ankle weights on when I was warming up over the hurdles. I took second in the event, and after the race, I was feeling very lightheaded. I was thinking to myself, my period must be getting ready to start, because I just feel so funny right now. I didn't say anything to Earnest about how I was feeling. I just continued running, but instead of my time improving, I was coming in at slower times, and jumping distances that I hadn't

33

seen since I was in high school. I remember when I first met Earnest's mom, the first thing she asked me was, "Are you guys using protection?" I was like, "What, we aren't even having sex", and Earnest kicked my leg under the table and shook his head like, she's asking, because she already knows the deal.

So, mid October rolls around, and I am having these horrible headaches, and to top it all off, my period has not started. Then, Earnest says to me one morning, "You are pregnant." I was in complete denial; I was like, "Why would you say that to me? That is not funny." I remember going to the health office that was on campus. I was explaining my symptoms to the doctor, trying to convince myself that I was just fighting a cold or flu bug or something. She said, "Let me do some blood work on you, and I will be back in with you shortly." It was the longest wait in the world, and on top of that, as if I was not stressed enough, that horrible feeling of dying was creeping back up again. I was like oh, this is really it, I am about to have a mental breakdown.

After what seemed like an eternity, the nurse comes back to the room. She didn't even try to beat around the bush, she was like, "Yep...you are definitely pregnant, and almost at the end of your first trimester." She hands me a card and says, "Here, we send all of the athletes here; you are still early enough to get an abortion. I already made an appointment for you; all you have to do is show up." I was speechless. Obviously I wasn't a saint, judging by the situation I was in, but I knew that having an abortion just didn't sit well with me. But my conviction was not strong enough to overrule the reality that I was sent here to fulfill my commitment to this college. I was on a full ride scholarship and my education was paid for; all I had to do was run, help my team win, and my degree was right around the corner. All of the people that believed in me would be so disappointed; so many expected so much more from me. Even the nurse had it all laid out for me. I felt so overwhelmed, but decided that I was going to the appointment.

It was a long bus ride home that day for me, and interestingly enough, I was doing my best to summon the detach defense, so that I would not allow myself to even acknowledge that I was pregnant. I decided I was not going to tell anyone, and I was going to pretend like nothing was going on. My stomach was still flat and I had not put on any weight. In fact, I had lost weight, so I could manage my way through this challenge on my own. If I ignored the entire situation, I wouldn't get emotionally attached, and I decided that once I got the abortion done, I was going to break up with Earnest, not date, and stay abstinent until I graduated from college.

Now the appointment was a few weeks out, and the nurse sent me home with all the check points of going through with the procedure. I was sick to my stomach when it highlighted that I must be accompanied by someone who could drive me. I really did not want to tell my girlfriend Katie. I knew I could depend on her, but I also knew she was very good friends with Earnest; they are like brother and sister. I thought, maybe this time she will not tell Earnest, because she will understand where I was coming from. Little did I know, Earnest already knew the deal without me even having to say anything to him, but he didn't tell me he talked to Katie? A few days before my appointment, Katie and I talked. She said, "Fahren, Earnest said that he would have had 4 children by now, but the girls he dated had abortions without even giving him the option to be a father. I am just asking you to consider his feelings; that's all. He can't stop you, and he probably won't, but just think about it." I heard her talking, but I didn't want to hear what she was saying. I was already emotionally detaching from Earnest; I just could not have a baby right now.

The night before the appointment, I just tossed and turned. When I woke up that morning, I just struggled to get out of the bed. I was sitting on the edge of the bed, and as clear as day, I heard this voice like it was coming from within my inner soul. "You are going to keep this baby girl." I want to say it sounded like my Grandma Cooper, but it was something that had never happened before. The strangest peace came over me; it was gentle. I was not confused. I just surrendered to the voice, and I said "Ok". I wondered if this was the Holy Spirit my grandmother had told me about when I went to see her?

I managed to finish out my sophomore year, but it was hard. I was so ashamed. My entire life direction had been interrupted. If I would have thought things through, or trusted someone enough to talk through my situation, I would have made better decisions concerning continuing my education. I was so deflated; I never returned my junior year. I just gave up. I didn't even think I was capable of giving up, but I did in this case, and it changed something in me. I could have redshirted my sophomore year, and returned to run for three more years, but I just gave up, and after that moment of letting go, I never felt like a champion again. I knew the road ahead of me was not going to be easy, because it no longer was about me; I had to die to myself, and make room for a new little person who, little did I know, was going to teach me how to truly love, from my heart.

My beautiful baby girl was born in May of 1993. I know her arrival actually saved my life and set me on a direction that I am not sure I would have ever taken. I would just stare at her, amazed that she came from me, that she was my baby, and then reality set in that I am now a mother. Emotionally, I felt alone; unprepared, but I wasn't alone in support from Earnest or my adoptive mom. Earnest was with me the entire time. If there is one thing he never loses focus or commitment on, it's his children. We decided that we were not going to get married just because we had a child. We had to work through some things and be completely sure that we were ready for 100 % commitment to each other. We knew we adored each other, and he was an excellent father, so I knew that our daughter would never have to worry about not having a relationship with her dad.

Chapter 6

Salvation Experience
~set aside my shame and confessed His name, by Faith I look
ahead~

Romans 10:9
*"that if you confess with your mouth the Lord Jesus and
believe in your heart that God has raised Him from the dead,
you will be saved."*

   I wish I could tell you that my salvation experience came with
a lot of bells and whistles, instant prosperity, and healing. I
believe this is the case for some, but it was not the case for me. I
was a young mother, and was blessed to have such great support
from both my family and Earnest's family. Earnest's mom would
encourage Earnest and I to go to church with her. I was just not
ready, and neither was Earnest, or more like, we thought we were
not ready. Earnest and I were pregnant with our second child, and
we still were not married. We thought we were doing okay. I

stayed home, while he worked, but something was definitely missing. We still really weren't fulfilled. I attributed my un-fulfillment to my sudden halt of no longer going to school and running track; it was the oddest feeling.

One day, you are at the PAC-10 championships, doing what you do best, and the next moment you are a mother. It was the most abrupt change of direction I've ever experienced. For someone who does not like sudden change, I did not quickly recover from that. I realize now that I really didn't emotionally know how to handle my situation, and being the private person that I am, I never reached out for emotional support or direction. I definitely had a pattern of holding on to things that have hap-pened to me, and one of my biggest challenges was learning how to let go of the past. Even more importantly, I didn't have a personal relationship with Christ to develop the Faith I needed to weather the storm.

We decided to take Earnest's mom up on her offer, and we went to her church. It was a predominantly African American church, located in the inner city of Seattle, WA. I had been traditionally raised Church of Christ. I was strictly taught, and learned that instruments should never be used in church, that you do not pray with the evidence of the Holy Spirit, which is speak-ing in tongues, and that you don't tithe, just give whatever God placed on your heart to give. I was never given any scripture that actually backed these beliefs up, but I was young and didn't read God's Word for myself. I just took whatever the preacher said, and that was my scripture.

So, imagine my conflict when I visited this church and they did all three. I thought I was going to be struck down with lightning from the Lord just for being inside the building. I could not even stay for the entire service; I was so uncomfortable. I had to do some serious soul searching to figure out what I did believe, as opposed to what I was taught, or else I was definitely going to have issues. Was I going to cast off my old way of thinking and try something different, or just live life, treating people nice, doing good works, taking care of my babies, and hoping that in itself would be enough to get me to heaven?

My husband loved the church and wanted to go back, even though we weren't exactly living a "Christian" life. I even remember a couple of times, I would smoke a joint before I went to service just because I thought it would relax me, and the two times I did that, the Pastor would be teaching on your body being the temple of the Holy Spirit. I was like, is God really paying that much attention to me that He would call me out like that? I still would do it, but I just didn't do it before church.

Over some time, I actually started listening to what the Pastor talked about, and he would speak on practical, everyday life stuff. I still didn't read the Bible, and the music thing was still a bit agitating, but the uneasiness finally let up. I was drawn to the teaching more than the atmosphere. The leaders were a bit stuffy, and I found it hard to really connect, but the teaching kept me anchored. I was learning that God's Word is a constant; it never changes, but is always current and relevant if you believe it and do what it says. I learned that growing up in church didn't mean that you were saved. Like my Pastor, Casey Treat, says today, "Sitting in a garage, won't turn you into a car." I think I was really trying to turn into a Christian.

It was 1994, and I was pregnant with our second daughter at the time. The Pastor asked this very necessary and relevant question. Have you confessed with your mouth, and believed in your heart that Jesus is the Lord of your life? I felt like I was the only one in the church, and that the spotlight was on me. I started thinking, I've never done that. I was always told I was saved, but I had never said those words. I remember being around 7 years old, and my adoptive mom scheduling my baptism, and I just about beat up everyone around me, because I was afraid of the water. I kept racking my brain, over and over, trying to figure out if I had actually said those words. I knew I was going to have to make a decision to choose a different life.

I didn't even look at Earnest; I closed my eyes thinking that maybe I can just say it from where I was sitting and do it inconspicuously, but I heard the Pastor say, "Be bold and come down to the front, so that we can pray with you." I can't tell you if my decision to want to say those words were based out of fear of going to hell, or that I really did want to change something? I think I fell somewhere in between.

So in that moment of the Pastor asking that question, I started feeling overwhelmed with guilt about everything. I was beginning to have all of these negative thoughts on why I didn't deserve to go up and be prayed for. I am living with my boyfriend, we have two kids together, I gave up on going to school and disappointed everyone, I don't trust people, I still don't really feel this music in the church thing, people are going to stare at me with my big 'ole pregnant belly, I'm really not a good person, I have some things I still like to do…and the thoughts just went on, and on. I had talked myself out of salvation, when I felt someone grab my hand. I didn't even know I was crying and sweating; I was a complete mess! Earnest says, "I will go with you."

I confessed Jesus as my Lord and Savior, even in the midst of all of those negative thoughts; I did it. I definitely felt something change in my heart. It was a process; however, because my Spirit was saved, but I still struggled. I kept feeling like I was missing something; like there should have been a next step. It was like, I got prayed for, and I truly meant that prayer of salvation, but that was it. It felt different, but I didn't look different or act different.

As a young girl, I adapted to my surroundings, kind of like a chameleon changes color to hide in their surroundings. That's what I did. I would observe the behavior of church people, and then mimic what they did. I figured I could fake it until it became real for me. I just assumed that I would be able to magically overcome worldly habits, things like smoking weed or going out. I was thinking, ok, I will be set free from all the things that are not good for me, and don't get me wrong, this can be the case, but it was not my case. I wanted to stop, but not really stop yet. It was like this tug of war, and I was stuck in the middle of it. I was not going to really give effort to change something that I really didn't want to change.

I had years, and years of heartache and cover up that I needed to deal with. I honestly did not know how to truly love and feel from my heart; I was so used to shielding it. I didn't realize the harder I became, the harder it was for me to recover when I was hurt. It's hard to put a shattered heart back together if it's been broken into many pieces. If I did not learn how to forgive and let go, I had the potential of shattering my heart to a point of no return. And so began my slow process of walking this life of Faith out.

Chapter 7

Awakening Gifts
~a call to prepare, not do~

2 Timothy 1:6a (NKJV)
"Therefore I remind you to stir up the gift of God..."

Earnest and I married, 6 months later, after our second daughter was born. I noticed that Earnest had this zeal that had not set in for me yet. He immediately began serving in the church; he loved the video ministry, and really loved working with cameras and with the security team. He had a great job that he absolutely loved, helping people find jobs for a non-profit organization. Spiritually, I just matured much slower than he did. I know when I gave my life to the Lord, I believed it with my heart, and the words I spoke were genuine, but the hardest thing for me to do was to understand that the Love of Christ was unconditional. Everything about my life, and the things that I encountered and experienced were based on conditions. Someone always wants something in return for something. So, reading the scriptures that talked about having no condemnation or guilt was just not logical to me. I could not figure it out, especially that in order to be saved; you had to believe by Faith.

Faith for me came and went. I would be strong in it one day, and then completely doubtful the next. I still held onto this security of at least having some idea of where I am going or what is coming up the road. I just didn't have the patience or courage to step into something that I couldn't see some sort of security in. I was still cautious when approaching relationships, and Earnest and my now mother-in-law used to encourage me to develop friendships with young women around my age. I had the hardest time; I felt safer around older women, I felt like I related to them better. The women my age didn't even have kids, and were still enjoying newlywed or single life. I was a young mother, and my focus now was my family. I did, however, start to serve in the church; thinking ok, I am going to do something that I enjoy doing, so I will sing in the choir.

I've always been a writer, as I mentioned earlier. Lyrically, poetically, short stories, thoughts, and revelations; I am more comfortable communicating on paper. I had all of my children by now, and was stirring up this love for music again. The music minister at the church was actually the reason I really started to become confident again in this area of my life. He was also a gospel recording artist, a songwriter, and worship leader. I used to sing with the choir when I was a little girl, but it was always accapella, as I mentioned.

I think back now, and I realize the benefit of being able to sing in pitch without music; it really trained me vocally without me realizing it. My singing voice was different from when I was younger, however. After I had all of my children, it was like my voice changed. I naturally began to fall in the lower alto and tenor range, when I was easily a high alto singer for most of my youth. It was kind of depressing, and I just figured that my singing days were over. Trying to get used to this lower tone was a little embarrassing for me to say the least. My music minister encouraged me even the more. He was like, "You have a strong, great voice, and it's beautifully unique. I have not heard this in the gospel industry, so you should keep singing to develop your confidence. Don't try to sing like someone else; your sound is original, and will be hard to mimic; people remember unique voices."

That encouragement helped me re-initiate the love I have for writing and singing. I did have some experiences that created some set backs for me; I remember this one situation, like it was yesterday. I decided to take this music workshop that was being held. The director of this workshop was well known in the community as a choir director and music director. During one of her sessions, she was positioning people in choir sections. I just automatically headed toward the tenor section, and stood there. She looked at me and called me out, "No, you move; there is no such thing as a female tenor. You need to stop smoking cigarettes, so you can heal your vocal chords." I was so embarrassed, because I was not a smoker, and my first thought was to give her a piece of my mind, but it probably would have resulted in a physical fight, and I didn't want to be known as the feisty girl who started fighting in a church. Hurt feelings and all, I stepped out of the section, grabbed my things, and left. Obviously, I still needed some emotional healing concerning people's opinions.

After that, I dropped out of the choir for 6 months, but not only did the music minister keep encouraging me, but my husband began to really encourage me as well, so that was important for me. My husband can't sing worth two cents, but he likes good singing, so for him to take and interest in me and music was a big deal. So, I began not just singing in choir again, but the music minister added me onto the praise team. He eventually helped me to put together my first music demo project, and connected me to two talented producers from the area.

I was proud of my little CD demo, and wanted to take it further and record a full album. Unfortunately, I didn't succeed in that; it was a crash and burn. I didn't understand the details of the music industry, recording, how much it costs, and everything in between. I just could not sustain the costs, and didn't have proper artist management, but I learned my lesson.

Looking back, I am glad that I didn't record a full album at that time. I just was not ready spiritually, emotionally, or as an artist. I confused my call to prepare with a call to go out and do. I stressed everyone out; my self and my family. I got so focused on creating a product that I lost sight of my first love, writing God's music and delivering it so that people would come to know Him through Jesus. I decided to take my hands off and let go. It wasn't worth losing my family over for sure. I settled in my spirit that if this was God's plan for my life, then it will come to pass. I don't know when, but I just know it will. I'm so glad I did, because a few years later, God brought the opportunity back around again, and it was a wonderful experience.

Chapter 8

Holy Spirit Healing
~your comfort comes when nobody else can~

John14:16a (KJV)
"And I will pray the Father, and he shall give you another
Comforter..."

Periodically, the pastor would call on people who wanted to receive the gift of the Holy Spirit, but I was too embarrassed to go down, only because I would hear other people pray so boldly in the Spirit. It was like they had studied it as a second language. When they would pray, it just sounded plain old scary to me. I am a slow processor, and it took me another year before I made the matter of fact decision that I was going to ask for this gift. I remember a series of events that literally set me on this pathway to get to a place of receiving the power of God's Spirit.

Sadly, I was still trying to kick my marijuana habit. I joke about this now, but I seriously felt like it was from the earth; how could it be bad for you? I had cut it down quite a bit, but I still would take a puff here and there. Additionally, I had not told Earnest about my episodes of feeling like I was dying, but one day it revealed itself to him in an un-cool way.

One night, Earnest and I were at his brother's apartment, and we were hanging out playing dominoes and listening to music. A few people were puffing on what I thought was the oddest looking joint. I hadn't seen anything like it before. Earnest warned me, "Look if you smoke that, it's stronger than what you are used to. It's called a blunt." I was like, "I got this boy; watch out, I will be ok." So I did. I took a long deep drag, and I thought my lungs, heart, and everything in between were coming up and out, because I was coughing so hard. I got myself under control, and I said to myself, "I am so done doing this."

So, after about fifteen minutes, that feeling of dying came back, only magnified one hundred times. I walked over to Earnest, in panic, "Earnest, my heart won't stop beating", and he said, "Fahren, that's a good thing; you don't want your heart to stop beating." I was like "No, you don't understand, it's beating really hard; can't you hear it?" Earnest looked at me and instantly knew I was going to start acting out. I'm sure he was thinking, "Oh Lord, here we go!" He kept his cool however and said, "Come here Fahren, come here." He took me over to the corner of the room and he said, "Just take a deep breath." I was like, "I'm dying. I can't breathe. My heart is hurting; it's beating too hard, I'm dying." Earnest said, "Fahren, you are messing my high up; come out here on this patio and get some air."

So, he had to escort me to the patio, because my head was spinning; everything was in slow-motion, and I was certain I was going to die that night. Earnest did everything to try and calm me down, all the way up to having me do jumping jacks outside. Everyone in the house was like, "What is wrong with her, is she ok?" Earnest said, "I'm taking you home." On the way home, I prayed…yes I sure did, I prayed. I was like, "Lord, if I live after tonight, I promise I will never smoke weed again." That night, I kicked my marijuana smoking habit. I tried to sneak it in here and there, but every time I would even smell it, I would begin to feel that horrible feeling that I was dying, so I just stayed away from people who even smoked it.

I remember going to the doctor and getting the nerve to talk to her about this feeling I was having; this feeling of dying. I explained to her my symptoms, and she asked me, "Are you under a lot of stress, or have you been through some sort of traumatic experience?" Instantly, I assumed that she was going to say that I was catching schizophrenia. That this was it, I was turning into a mentally ill woman.

So, I almost didn't hear her next phrase, when she said, "It sounds like you are dealing with panic or anxiety attacks." It's where an overwhelming sense of fear comes on suddenly. She said, "It's frightening and very unsettling, but it's harmless and does not cause any physical harm to you." She went on to say that they are usually a trigger from something else, and to think about getting some therapy to discuss things that were on my mind, or that I was dealing with.

I remember one evening I thought I heard my husband praying, only it sounded like another language. Now, I would hear people at church speak in "tongues", which is evidence of being filled with the Holy Spirit. I was taught in my childhood church that only certain people had this gift, and that it was not for everyone. I had never heard it done, and just figured that no one in that church had the gift.

Initially, when we started going to this new church ministry, along with my issue with music, I had to push through my thoughts on hearing people pray this way as well. So, when I heard my husband doing it, I asked him, "When did you learn how to do that?" He said, "I've always known how to do it." I was like, "Only appointed people can do that; have you been appointed?" He answered, "No Fahren, it's a gift that God gives you; all you have to do is ask for it." He said, "When we went up to get saved, did you ever look at the pamphlet that they handed to you?" I was like, "No not really; I mean I read the first part, but that's it." He disappeared for a moment and came back in with this small blue book. He turned it to the chapter about the power of the Holy Spirit, and how important it is to the Christian walk. I felt like maybe this is what was missing, why I really couldn't breakthrough the way I really wanted to.

My husband's words about this Holy Spirit power resonated in my mind, and I asked myself an internal question, "Can the Holy Spirit help me overcome this anxiety?" It was as if something spoke to my heart, and said, "Just ask for it and see." When I got home from my doctors appointment, I looked for the blue book my husband gave me, and turned to the page that talked about how to receive the gift of the Holy Spirit. I was sitting upstairs reading the book, and my children were downstairs playing. As I was about to go through this process, my oldest daughter ran up the stairs frantic, "Mom...Lil Earnest is chocking." I jumped up and ran to the door, looked down the stairs, and there was my son; hands around his throat, not making a sound, and staring up at me in sheer horror. I can't tell you if I touched one stair, but before I knew it, I had picked my son up, turned him around, and smacked him right in the middle of his back, and out popped this jolly rancher he had been sucking on. I brought him upstairs, and just held him. I was shaken, and he could feel me trembling, and he just hugged me.

Right then, I just started crying, and then my crying turned into sobbing. By then, my girls had come upstairs, and were not sure what to do. It was as if something was speaking to my heart, and asking me, "Are you ready for this Holy Spirit power you've been looking for? All you have to do is ask." I just starting praying, "Yes God, I receive the Holy Spirit. Yes, I want this for me, I need help." I put my son down, and felt like I could not get low enough to the floor. I had finally gotten down, and was laying flat on my stomach with my face on the floor, and right then, the evidence of the Holy Spirit hit me, and I began to speak in tongues.

My oldest daughter came over, and I could feel her hand on my back. She didn't say a word; she just sat there, while I was lying on my face. When I got up off of that floor, I just knew that I was no longer going to have panic attacks. I didn't need therapy, I didn't need someone to lay a hand on me; it was the power from the Spirit of the living God that delivered me. I was willing to let it go, and in my surrender, He took it. I have not had a panic attack since then. That was 1998, and this new zeal for the things of God just overtook me, and it became my primary focus of everything that I did.

Chapter 9

Renewing
~You prosper, as your soul prospers~

3 John 1:2
"Beloved, I pray that you may prosper in all things and be in health, just as your soul prospers."

My mother-in-law has always been a part of my life, and really was the quiet wisdom I needed. I swore she was some sort of prophet or something, because she always knew what was going on. She lived with us for many years, and provided support, spiritual mentoring, training, and love in raising my children and teaching me how to be a woman who took care of her home and her husband. Homemaking was just not my favorite thing to do. To be honest, I didn't have to do it as a child. My adoptive mom hired maids to clean, so I just knew that when I grew up and got married, I was going to do the same thing. It freed up time for her to focus on other things, and I really liked that concept. Only problem is, my husband is a southern man; born and raised in

Chattanooga, TN. He grew up with his grandmother and his mother as the matriarchs of the home. So, in his mind, you are not a woman if you don't know how to care for your home, point blank.

Now, I knew how clean up. I just didn't want to do it, and when I did, I did it when I was ready. I also was still trying to overcome this feeling of not having financial security. It took many years of patience from my mother-in-law and husband to help me work through these areas in my life; it was not; however, without some intense moments. When I started working my first job, every time I would get paid, I would take money and stash it, and I would not tell my husband. From the time Earnest and I were married, he had this odd pattern of employment. He would never work for more than 2 years on a job with out being laid off. At first, I was really positive, and full of faith. We tithed, and I know that this really helped us through some difficult times and kept the enemy from overtaking us, but keeping it real; losing his income put us into some tough financial hardships.

I was not used to having to move because I couldn't pay my rent. I never knew what it was like to not have food or my basic necessities. I tell you, I really know what it's like to have plenty and what it is like to not have a dime. Our lights would get cut off, heat shut off, cupboards empty, and barely able to pay the rent. We moved nine times, and had to file bankruptcy to keep our home, and ended up having to sell it anyway. Our marriage relationship was so stretched that if one more disaster had of happened, we would have both snapped. I would get some modeling gigs on the side, and had a 401K investment, but I would have to always drain out my accounts to pull us out of financial troubles. Being in lack just didn't set right with me at all. If I want to buy makeup, or get my kids a pair of much needed shoes, I wanted to be able to do that.

I have never been a person of expensive taste, and I don't like a lot of expensive jewelry. I am always looking for the best bargain. I felt like I had no control over his job situation, but if I work every day, I refuse to walk around broke and broke down. I never made my husband feel like he was not a man; however, my way of dealing with it was to stash cash. The only problem is, I would have to scheme and figure out how to calculate what I wanted to keep, and that was plain old deception, which will destroy a marriage altogether.

I think that Earnest threatened to leave me about seven times over these issues. Even with this, it was a process to overcome, and without God in the middle of all of it, I don't even know if we would still be together. So, as a side note to my married readers, you and your spouse are one. If you can't share with each other and be open and honest about all areas of your life, you will have major challenges. Trust is earned and not demanded or controlled. Just thought I would throw that in there.

By 2001, my mother-in-law had begun visiting another church. She never told us why initially. Earnest and I had begun to sense some spiritual changes in the ministry we were in also, but we could not put our finger on it. I was, by now, involved with the music ministry. I sang on the praise team; never as a leader or anything like that, just as a background vocalist, and I was comfortable there. I had made friends; I had even worked on a music Demo. I noticed Earnest didn't want to go to church as much anymore, and when I would ask him what was going on, he would say, something is just not right. My commitment in a sense clouded my judgment, but I just began to pray, "Lord, show me what I need to see; my mother-in-law is visiting other churches and my husband doesn't go anymore, am I missing something?"

That night, I had the craziest dream. I dreamed that I was singing with the praise team at the church; at the same time, I was sitting out in the congregation. I could hear what sounded like someone narrating what was happening on the pulpit platform. The narrator would say, "Look at the team", and I would look, and instantly I could see the manifestation of their praise going up; it looked like little clouds would come out of their mouth when they sang, and began to float up. Then the narrator would say, "Look up." So, I looked up and saw a glass ceiling over the pulpit platform. I could see through the glass, and what looked like all of these gifts, and prizes; it looked like answered blessing just piled high on top of the glass.

The narrator made this statement, "When Praise and Worship goes up it must be in Spirit and in Truth; God then, in accepting the Praise, rains down His blessings on His people." The narrator then asked, "Why then is the praise not releasing the blessing?" I was horrified; I looked at myself singing on stage, and watched the puffs of clouds coming out of my mouth, floating up toward the glass ceiling, but never making an impact to the glass. It was the same for all of the other praise team members as well. The narrator continued, "Why are these blessings being held up? God is not holding them up. Is this praise and worship true enough to break that ceiling and release those blessings?" Then right in my ear, I heard the narrator say, "No, it is not. God is moving you to a place where you can experience real worship, and see the manifestation of what happens in true praise. It's time to go", and then I woke up.

I didn't even doubt that this was the word of the Lord. I was so hurt and I repented and asked God to forgive me for not giving Him my worship, in spirit and in truth. It was never the primary focus; I worried more about sounding good and looking good, and learning the next harmony part, and how cool this run is or how great a singer this person is that I absolutely missed what I was supposed to get. I told Earnest about my dream, and he said, "Fahren, I felt that a year ago, and more than just that; God spoke to you in your language; your heart is your praise, so He spoke to you this way, and showed you what was enough to get your attention. I was going to say something, but you were so committed to that ministry that I knew you would not really hear me, so I just backed off and asked God to speak to your heart."

I knew then that it was time to move; we had stopped growing and we were going through some peculiar attacks and things that we should have easily overcome, but suffered more loss than gain, in more ways than one. I knew it was God who had definitely rescued us, because less than 5 years later, that ministry was no more, and many people were hurt and fell away from the Faith as a result.

Once again, we were invited to a new church by my mother-in- law. It was the same ministry that printed up that little blue book I received when I gave my life to Christ. Not only that, but my husband had received a book as a gift written by the Pastor of this ministry we were visiting. The book was called *Renewing the Mind*[1] by Dr. Casey Treat. Today, he is our spiritual father, and his amazing ministry, *Christian Faith Center*[2], is part of the reason we are still standing today. We had his book in our home, not realizing the treasure it held. The whole message on Renewing the Mind was exactly what we needed to hear, and what we should have heard when we gave our lives to Christ in 1995. Yes, we were saved, walked by Faith, prayed, paid our tithes, and changed some of our bad behavior, but never really dealt with renewing things. We just learned how to pile things on top of pain: un-resolve, un-forgiveness, and trust issues. It was only by God's grace that He loved us enough to show us that we were not in the right place to receive renewal.

There were many signs along the way- hint, my in-ability to truly get settled and receive fully the love of Christ. Something that I later realized was abandonment issues, or the fear of being settled in one spot. Other signs were not reading the Word for myself, and getting it so into my spirit that the God's Word was my response to everything, my decision making and how I handled my finances; just no wisdom, and didn't really seek it out. I was still trying to control, instead of being led. My intentions to choose Life and to live by Faith were true and very real; to believe in something, a Christ, God, and the presence of His Spirit were true and very real, and by God's divine appointment.

I had the tools in me and the weapon of God's Word at my reach, but did not know how to properly use it. I lacked, as a baby Christian, discipleship to help me drink milk first to protect my spiritual digestive system, and ease it into digesting solids. I finally realized at that moment that I missed a very important step in the process of living by Faith. I didn't fully surrender some things, and I learned that God will never go against my will. His love never changes, His miracle working power never changes, His Word never changes, and His promises never change; it was I that needed to change.

The moment I walked into this new church, I knew it was where I was supposed to be. Earnest felt the same, and we felt this for our family. It was very similar as far as look and structure of our previous church, but the atmosphere and spirit of the church was completely different. It was something about the Worship that just drew me in. It was absolutely the polar opposite of my taste in music. I love contemporary, urban gospel music; it's what took me in to the throne room, as people say, and it still takes me there.

Of course, now God has expanded my genre to include all sorts of music, because I've learned that God music speaks the Word of God, and anyone can receive that; the delivery of it is one's preference. I wondered, "How on earth is God using rock music to draw me in." I realized that it wasn't the genre that drew me; it was the spirit of the worship that drew me. It was passionate, not perfect. Almost every song was sung in only two parts, hi and low; no tricky, cool parts, or rifts or anything. I was like, "Wow ok, I may not serve in this ministry, because I can't sing like that, but I don't mind lifting my hands and tapping into that spirit of worship along with the congregation."

More importantly, the Word that Pastor Casey brought was just so practical and easy to understand. He made learning God's Word practical, relatable, and fun. You know a great leader when they make being led fun and empowering. I not only listened to the Word, but I was always compelled to go back and read and gain deeper understanding for myself. I promised myself that never again would I give God selfish praise, or a "Look at me praise". I was always going to remind myself to make sure my praise pointed to Him, so that others can follow Him. I promised myself that my destiny and self-worth was no longer controlled by a man; not my husband, a pastor, my children, my parents, my background, my past, my sin; not anything. There are so many testimonies of the goodness of God, and how he brought me through, my marriage through, and my family through.

My husband and I could honestly jointly write a book together on our experiences and perspectives on marriage, children, tests, and trials, because we have definitely earned our stripes. I knew that coming to Christian Faith Center was a God move. And I was resolute. I was not going to be moved; my cause was Christ, and no one could take my view off of that. After over a year of just sitting in the ministry, going to a two week membership class, and 6 weeks of discipleship classes, I was ready to live a lifestyle of Faith, through Christ.

Chapter 10

A Walk Through the Valley
~the great I AM, my source and strength to stand~

Exodus 3:14 (KJV)
"And God said to Moses, "I AM WHO I AM." And He said,
"Thus you shall say to the children of Israel, 'I AM has sent me
to you.'"

My adoptive parents were getting older. At one point, my mom and dad were in the same hospital room. It was just very hard for me to see two people who have always been the strongest humans on the earth; full of life, giving and serving their community, and always offering a helping hand side by side in the hospital. My parents suddenly lost their home, while their affairs were being handled by an executor over their estate. They had to be moved into an assisted living facility, and were only able to take what they could get out of the home at the time; it was devastating for both my mother and father. Their goal was to be able to leave something for their children, and they were unable to do that. So, my parents asked me and Earnest to take over as executor of their estate. Their finances were in complete disarray, and there was no way I would be able to track and figure out the trail of all of it. My parents understood my apprehension, so my dad asked his cousin to take over as executor, and it was the best decision for all of us.

I made sure that I visited my parents, helped clean their apartment, and took them where they needed to go. I remember I had visited my parents one afternoon, and my dad started talking to me about his funeral. I told him, "Why are we talking about this; I don't want to do this right now," and he was like, "I just want you to know that I am probably going to die before your mom, and here is what I have already taken care of." I just started crying. I remember going into the room with my mom, while Earnest was still there with my dad. I could hear Earnest praying with my dad. When he was done, Earnest gestured for me to go; I kissed my mom and dad, and left.

As we left, Earnest said, "Did you know that your dad had never confessed Jesus as His Lord and Savior?" I was like, "No." This whole time, I assumed that my dad was saved and didn't go to church, because he just didn't like going, even though he had a heart of gold and didn't treat people bad. I just totally took that for granted all of these years. Earnest continued, "You don't have to worry about it, I prayed the prayer of salvation with him just now, and I know he believed it and received it with all of his heart."

My dad was diagnosed with congestive heart failure, and his doctor put him on a strict renal diet. He had been a smoker from the time he was 15 years old, and it was the main reason why his health deteriorated. He could not drink too much water, and we had to count every gram of sodium on packages before we could buy them. A week later, my dad was in the hospital. His heart was failing.

I remember Earnest and I went to the hospital to see him, and he asked Earnest to take his rings (my dad loved jewelry), and Earnest just could not do it. Instead, he took them and put them in a zip lock bag and gave them to my mom. A few days later, that baggy came up missing in their little apartment. Earnest wished he would have taken my dad's rings home, and that still bugs him to this day. My parents could no longer stay in assisted living, and we had to find a fully skilled nursing facility to place them in. The plan was that once my dad was released from the hospital, we would move him in, and get a room that both of my parents could share. I remember the day we brought him to the new nursing facility. It was nice, and I was very adamant about that. We got him settled in his room, and all he kept asking was when "Dutchess" (my mom's nickname) was going to come. I kept reassuring him that we were moving her in, in just a couple of days. He was so excited.

My adoptive dad and Earnest had a great relationship. Those who know my husband know he has this gift of making people laugh, and I remember him talking to my dad, and he would say, "Mr. Thomas, I know you don't like this food; let's boycott the cafeteria and get some real soul food cooks up in this place"…my dad just laughed, because he strongly detested any food that was not soul food. The director had me come in and sign some paperwork while I was there. There was this form that asked a question about resuscitation, and if I wanted my dad to be worked on in the event his heart stopped. Now my dad was perfectly clear about not being brought back to life, but I had the hardest time selecting that box. I felt like me signing this was giving them the permission to let him die. It was so hard. After I finished up the paperwork, we headed out to finish packing up my mom for her move.

I remember Earnest whispering something into my dad's ear, and he just laughed. I kissed him, and was like ok daddy, I will see soon, I am going to get your wife, and he just smiled. His room window was facing the parking lot that we were parked in. We could see him sitting on the side of his bed, looking out at the window at us. I remember waving to him, and him giving his head nod to acknowledge me back. That was the last day I saw him; I got the call around nine o'clock the next morning that he had passed away.

It was my first experience dealing with the death of someone who was that close to me. We didn't have a very deep father-daughter relationship, but I still loved him for being so willing to take me into his home and raise me as his child. My mom was so hurt; they had been through so much together, and loved each other. I was so sad that she didn't get a chance to see him before he passed.

We had to move my mom into a different nursing facility, which just bugged me. Her condition just needed more medical care than I could physically provide. She had been on dialysis for many years, and I would sit with her during her treatment days, three times a week. She could not walk, and could no longer eat solids. She had suffered from a stroke, and so her ability to use her hands was very limited; she had to be fed. She was a very quiet woman. She did not complain much at all. Even if something was wrong, she didn't talk about it. I would go with her to her doctor appointments; sometimes riding the shuttle with her, and sometimes following her shuttle bus to the appointments in my car. She was my baby; I just adored and loved her. I knew that I was going to adjust some things in my life, to make sure she had what she needed.

Chapter 11

Finality of Letting Go
~never thought how letting go could be so freeing~

Philippians 3:13 (KJV)

"Brethren, I do not count myself to have apprehended; but one thing I do, forgetting those things which are behind and reaching forward to those things which are ahead..."

I will never forget the day that I let go of hiding my past. It happened in a way that I would have never imagined. It was November of 2005, and my church puts on an annual Women's Conference. This was my first time serving in the conference as part of the praise team. I was working at the time, and so I didn't plan on taking any days off to attend the morning/afternoon sessions, but planned to sing with the team for the evening services. The woman who was over the music team called me the night before, and asked was there anyway that I could be available to sing at one of the morning sessions; there was a specific song that she wanted me to lead that morning. I told her that I didn't think I would be able to at such short notice for work, but that I would try and see if I could work something out.

After I got off of the phone with her, I gave my manager from work a call, and asked if I could have the morning off, and just come in a little later, that there was something that I needed to do. I thought that she was going to ask me more specific questions, but she just said, "Sure, I will see you a little later tomorrow." I was like, "Ok, that definitely was not expected, but praise the Lord!"

So the next morning, we sound checked and I decided to step out and meet some new ladies that I've seen at church, but didn't really know their names. Praise and Worship that morning was anointed, and when I stepped forward to lead the last song, something just began to stir in me. I will never forget the song; it was called "Now That I Know", written by an amazing worship leader by the name of Eddie Hunt.

As I ministered the song, it was as if all 2,000 plus women that were in the building disappeared, and it was just me talking directly to my God. "Now that I know who You are, the joy that Your life brings, I worship You my King. Now that I know who You are, Your love's so overwhelming, and forever my heart sings Jesus." I could hear the Spirit of the Lord saying, you are going to break the shame and guilt of your past; it will no longer be a remnant in your life. I could physically feel this heaviness lifting off of me, and I felt like I was so light that I was going to lift right up off of the ground. When Praise and Worship was over, I could hear the Holy Spirit speak to my heart, and the words "You are going to share something that is not only going to break the shame and guilt off of you, but it's going to release bondage from other women that are here as well."

I am pretty confident of when I hear the Holy Spirit speaking, but I was not sure if I was really hearing correctly. I began to debate in my heart about what I had just heard in my spirit. I was like, "Oh no, no, no, Lord, You have the wrong sister this morning. I can't speak in front of people; I would not know what to say, and besides the Pastor does not know me like that, and she never just puts the mic in the hands of someone she doesn't have relationship with." The Holy Spirit spoke to my heart again, "I have already prepared the way, and when it is time, you will know what to say."

I am now shaking my head, and I bet people probably thought I was just so moved by the worship, which was good, but if they only knew that I was shaking my head telling the Holy Spirit, "No, I think You are mistaken; I am not the one, I am not ready." Now, I watched my Pastor coming up to the platform, and she did something I had never seen her do before. She began to hug all of the praise team members, starting from the opposite side I was standing on. I heard the Holy Spirit say, "When she gets to you, tell her you have something to share." I was like, "Are you kidding me; please don't make me do that Lord, please." I thought I was going to faint right there from hearing my heart beating so hard.

Thank goodness I was delivered from panic attacks, or else they would have been calling the aid care that morning! Finally, she get's to me, and I say to her, "Pastor, I have something on my heart that I want to share with the ladies". She was like, "Ok", grabbed my hand and pulled me to the front and announced to the ladies, "Fahren has something she wants to share", and put the microphone in my hand. I was like Holy Spirit, don't leave me now...and He didn't. I shared my testimony; something I had kept hidden from many of my church family.

I shared that day, in front of a room full of women that I did not know, about being born to a mentally ill mother, conceived in a mental institution, years of sexual abuse, along with identity and trust issues. I shared that, but more importantly shared that through it all, through the process of healing, God took all that the enemy meant for my destruction, and turned it around for His Glory. I left this with the ladies; "I am here today, because of God's grace, His Love, His patience, His covering, and protection. I could have easily been a different woman, but because from the womb He called my name, I have a purpose. If He can do it for me, I know that He can do it for you."

When I finished, everyone stood to their feet and just clapped and praised God. I remember we had a special guest Pastor speaking that morning from Abundant Life Ministries[3] in England. Her message was "What is in your Cupboard?"[4] Her message spoke directly to my heart, and reminded that in me are all of the tools, gifts, and talents to do what God has called me to do. It was as if God had set this day up, specifically for me to experience just how much He loves and cares about me as an individual.

After service, the Pastor from England asked to speak to me, so I was taken back to a room to meet her. She told me, "You have a beautiful voice; anointed, but that is not the only thing in your cupboard. Your story is going to set people free; your music is the vehicle God is going to use to communicate your Story. Start writing and journaling your accounts and experience. It is going to be a process, you are going to have great challenges, but you will overcome, and out of it you will write the testimony.

The enemy is going to do everything in his power to throw you off track, but do not be afraid, God is with you, and you are going to write not for yourself, but for others who will go, or are going through what God has redeemed you from." I will never forget her words, because when I left that room, I grabbed a new member card, and I wrote down her prophetic Word; I still have it to this day.

I can't tell you how many women found me that day, and shared about the shame of sexual abuse, or rape, or mental illness that kept them in bondage, and how God used me to speak to them. Many of them dealt with un-forgiveness and realized that in order for them to begin the process of healing; they simply had to release their abuser by just forgiving.

I could go on with testimonies from that day to present, as I share my testimony, how many people have gone through the same thing, but did not know how to position themselves for deliverance and redemption. I learned that day to never argue with the Holy Spirit; He only communicates what the Father communicates, so when He speaks, just do what He says.

Chapter 12

Married with Children
~now I'm all grown up with my own~

Genesis 18:19a (NKJV)
"For I have known him, in order that he may command his children and his household after him, that they keep the way of the LORD..."

I have four beautiful children; three girls and one boy, and they are all about 2 years apart. I know this may sound cliché, and that every parent says this about their children, but seriously, God spoke to both Earnest and I about our children, and how they were going to grow up to do amazing things for the Kingdom of God. When each one of our children was born, Earnest would take them and lift them up into the air towards heaven and pray over them. It was touching, and it reminded me of a movie I remembered seeing called "Roots"[5]. The father, who was a slave, took his son, Kunta Kinte, and lifted him up to the Lord. That boy went on to become a mighty warrior, and delivered his people out of oppression.

I cried after I thought about how significant that was, and how much Earnest wanted to see his children live for the Lord. Its like, when you have kids, something in you says, I want them to know who they are in Christ at a young age, as soon as they are able to fully comprehend who He is. I thank God that we got it together before our oldest turned two years old, because we wanted to raise and teach them how to walk in relationship with him, and not just go to church like we did.

My mother-in-law was very instrumental in helping to lay down the strong spiritual foundation in our home. It's something about a Grandma's prayer, faith, and wisdom that is just effective. She taught me and my kids how to pray. I think right now, their prayer life is way more mature than mine was at their age. When the kids didn't feel well, they automatically knew to go lie down in grandma's bed, or go sit next to grandma; it was something about her faith that laid the framework of who my children are today.

One thing I can say is from the time our children could comprehend the joys and trials of life, we kept it real. We didn't hide them from the world; we schooled them on the world, and then directed them to the Word, where they could get equipped to live in the world. We used our life experiences to aid in directing them.

The older and more mature they became; the more things we shared. See, we didn't want our children to be so spiritually minded that they could not be any earthly good. We raised them to be diverse children; they attended private and public school; one that was predominately African American, and a few that were predominantly white. We lived in the most diverse area code in the nation for many years. We wanted to raise our children to not only be comfortable in their own skin, but to be comfortable around those who didn't look like them as well.

Many times, I watch children who try to fit in to another culture or group of people, all because they don't realize the uniqueness of which they are, and how powerful that alone can be. I wanted my kids to fully understand that knowing who you are and having the right heart when you do things is more important to God, and important to us. We were mindful and watchful to guard what went into our children's eyes and ears.

When they were babies up until they started school, we would turn on Jazz, Classical, and Gospel in their rooms at night. As they got older, we would introduce R&B, Hip-hop, Reggae, and everything in between. All of our children to this day are great lovers of all types of music, and we did that on purpose. I can say today that they all love God, have healthy self images, and are aware of their God given gifts and talents. They have a heart for their community, and for people that are less privileged. All of my children are gifted socially; they can naturally relate to people. We raised them to be these types of individuals, because in order to spread the Gospel, you need to relate to people. Sex Education was taught at home before they started to receive the world view of sex in school. We have had many conversations in our home about sex, it's meaning, and what God says about sex.

When our children got to the age to where they were mature enough to make life choices, they each determined on their own that they were going to keep themselves virgins until marriage. Of course, Earnest and I shared with them the negatives of giving your spirit (having sex) to someone you are not married to; the doors it opens up in your heart, spirit, and soul. Earnest and I shared our struggles that we had early on in our relationship, because our goal is to help detour them away from making the same mistakes we made, so that they will do their best to stay on God's path now, better than what we were able to do.

We realize they are going to make mistakes and that they will have seasons of challenge, but we are confident that the Word in them is their response to those situations and challenges. Faith is a choice, and you have to choose to walk by it every single day. They are your typical teenagers, and are by far not perfect. We correct when necessary, and support them continually. My husband is more of the disciplinary than I am, and we are ok with this. I remember we had a season with our two youngest children. It just seemed like if they said hi to each other, it would turn into an argument. I had begun to wonder if they even liked each other. I used to call them Tom and Jerry, because that's how they used to act with each other.

One day, I came home and they were arguing about who was supposed to do what chore and so on. So, my husband got up to see what was going on. I walked back to my room and the arguing had stopped. A few moments later, here comes Tom and Jerry, walking down the hallway, holding hands. I'm like, "What in the world are you guys doing?" They responded, "Daddy told us we had to hold hands for 30 minutes to figure out how to work together to get the chores done, without letting go." I was like, "Wow, I would have never thought to do that." Earnest always used creative and inventive disciplinary actions. I just follow his lead, and use his same techniques.

We love the season we are in with them right now, and we heard such horror stories about teenagers. We prepared ourselves, but also poured into them when they were younger. We established right away, when they were young, the behavior we wanted and didn't want to see. We have always talked to our children, prior to disciplinary action and just in everyday conversation. When we were going through tough times financially, we would sit our kids down and talk about it. Talk about how they can help us, by just adding their Faith to ours, and trusting in God's Word that He is the supplier of all of our needs.

Every Monday night is prayer night in our home, where we come together with personal prayer requests, and each person prays for another. We have taught them that praise and prayer and reading the Word of God is a daily lifestyle. Our children have been raised in church, yet when they received Jesus as their Lord and Savior, it was their decision; we didn't force them or make them. We figured if they can choose Christ, then they will be able to choose to obey and use His Word for all other choices in life that they will need to make. We want them to have a reverent fear and love of God; not be afraid of Him. I am so thankful that God entrusted me with such amazing kids. There is no way I would be the woman I am today if it were not for them.

Chapter 13

She's Gone, but Not Forgotten
~Follow me to L.O.V.E.~

2 Corinthians 5:8
*"We are confident, I say, and willing rather to be absent from
the body, and to be present with the Lord."*

In August of 2008, my mother had become very ill. She was
81 years old. The nursing home she was in recommended that I
put her into hospice, because she had stopped eating. She did not
want a feeding tube. I insisted that they run more tests on her, and
we found that she had caught an infection, so they were able to
treat it and I had began to bring foods that she liked to eat, and
she did ok. She was a diabetic all of her life, but for the most part
took very good care of herself. After she suffered a stroke and my
father passing, she went downhill very quickly. She developed
sores that her body just could not heal. I had been taking her to a
foot doctor that did their best to try and aid and speed the healing

Fahren J

of sores that were on her feet. She ended up losing her toe, but we were able get the other sores healed up. I was happy about that, and really confident that she would not lose any of her limbs due to diabetes. I had taken some time off of work to be with her, and I will never forget this day I went to visit her. It was very nice outside; she was in a wheel chair, so I decided that for this day, we would do our visit outside. I stopped and picked up some orange pop... (her favorite), and a CD player with some of my new music that I was working on. We sat outside in the warm sun; I gave her sips of orange pop, while she listened to the music through headphones. She just smiled, and I told her how much I adored and loved her. She told me that her favorite song was "He is God", a song I had actually written for a children's album, but never released, so I kept it for my new CD project.

The next day, I got a call from the nursing home; they told me that they had to admit my mom into the hospital for another infection. I almost thought it was my fault for bringing her outside in the sun; maybe it was too much for her. They told me that her leg had gone completely black, and that they were going to need to amputate it. The gang green from her leg had gotten into her bloodstream, and they were trying their best to treat it. I called up to the hospital, and found out that she was still in the emergency room. I called my sister and told her that mom was very sick and that we needed to get up to the hospital right away. She came and we drove up together.

Nothing could have prepared me for when I entered into her room. She was in a hospital bed. Her mouth was wide open, as if she was gasping for air. Her leg was black, and I could see this tube full of green fluid leading to a plastic bag and being released inside of it. I ran to her, and just started calling her name. I kept telling her, "I love you momma, I love you baby." It was obvious that she was in pain, because I could hear her moaning. I felt like she could hear me, but the pain she was in just seemed so overwhelming. Not even ten minutes after arriving, the doctor came in.

Very point blank, he was like listen, "She is not doing well. She has no circulation in this leg. Even if we were to amputate it, because of her age and the condition of her body right now, she may not make it through the surgery. Secondly, the infection from her leg is now in her blood stream. You see this tube full of green pus leading to this bag? That is her urine. The infection is so far advanced into her system that trying to treat it would be very rigorous on her already fragile body." The doctor continued, "Her body has had enough, it is tired, and it's going to keep breaking down. If this were my mother, I would not want to see her suffer, and would make these last days the most comfortable for her as much as possible."

Oh, I just lost it. I cried so hard, I almost could not breathe. Was he asking me to let my mother die? Please tell me he is not asking me this. Why do I have to make this decision, it's not right. I want her to live, I am going to tell you to do everything that you can to sustain her life, because I am not ready for her to go; I am going to be completely selfish in this decision. Immediately, the Holy Spirit spoke to my heart, and said, "Ask her if she is tired?" I looked at the doctors and nurses and asked them if they would give me a moment alone with my mom. After they walked out, I turned away from my mom for a moment, and just cried, cried, and cried. Once I got myself together, I walked up and grabbed her hand, and I just said, "Momma, I love you, but if you are tired, I will understand." (Now in my flesh that is not how I was feeling; what I wanted to say, is "Momma, these doctors are telling me to not give you anymore treatment; they are telling me to let you die", but I knew that was my selfishness talking, and that is not what they were saying at all, and definitely not what she needed or probably wanted to hear either). I could clearly hear her answer me through what seemed like unbearable pain, "Yes, I'm tired. I am ready to go see "Bop" (that was my dad's nickname). As soon as she said that, the Holy Spirit brought back to my remembrance a dream that I had a few months prior to this day. I am amazed at how God has a way of preparing you for tough times, if you continue to abide in Him.

In this dream, I was in a hospital room, and my mom was sitting in her wheelchair in the room. We were talking, and I remember her telling me to make sure I take care of myself, stay healthy, and always keep family first. She was telling me about things she wished she would have done differently when it came to family and how she managed her time. The first part of the dream really was a word of the Lord to me, because at the time, Earnest and I were having some heated discussions around this area of our lives. He was telling me that I was so busy serving at the church, and making it way too much of a priority to the point of stressing over it, that my home life had gotten out of whack. Earnest was like, "How can you serve at church, and your home is completely out of order?" Now my husband believes in serving God's kingdom and God's house, so I want to make that clear. What he had a challenge with was when the family suffered at the hands of it. Of course, he was right, and it was a truth pill that was hard for me to swallow at the time, but I knew that this dream was helping me to process this.

The dream continued, and I remember the door to the room was open and I could see out into the street. After we talked for quite sometime, this dark maroon Lincoln Navigator pulled up, and I could see a chauffeur in the driver's seat. He had on a white suite, with black sunglasses. The back door to the Navigator opened, and there was my dad sitting there; he looked really good, and had on some dark sun glasses. He waved to my mom, and said, "Come on "Dutchess" (my mom's nickname); it's time to go." My mom was so excited that she got up out of the wheelchair, and walked straight out of the hospital door and got into the backseat with my dad. They hugged for what seemed like an eternity. I don't think I had ever seen them hug like that in my life. Right before they pulled off, my mom called to me. She said, "Remember what I said lil girl", and they both told me that they loved me and that I would see them again. The door to the Navigator closed, and the car pulled off.

Even when the Holy Spirit brought this dream to my remembrance, I still found it hard to accept her answer, but I chose to obey her wishes. By this time, all of the doctors who had been instrumental in my mother's care had arrived, and through very hurt feelings, I communicated my mother's wishes, not mine. Every last doctor came to me individually and expressed their support of honoring my mother's wishes, and not prolonging the transition of what happens in old age, death. It was by far one of the biggest storms of my life.

This was the woman who took me into her home and loved me unconditionally, and in my eyes, was my mother, will always be my mother, and was the one assigned to me and I to her; all a part of God's bigger plan, not man's. My sister and I began the process of notifying friends and family. The moment they moved her into a private room, it was as if she was already at peace. I sang to her, I kissed her, and I held her hand. She showed no signs of pain whatsoever, so we did not even have to administer drugs that would keep her comfortable. That night, my husband and long time friend of our family, Will Roberts, came and sat with me. Though she never woke up, I knew she could sense I was there. Whenever I would whisper in her ear how much I loved her, she would respond, "I love you." Morning came, and we had received some visitors.

While my sister and I were in the room, the Chaplain walked in. We talked with her, and shared the background of our mom, and how much she meant to us; even the Chaplain cried, and told us she was so glad that she had a chance to meet the children of such a giving woman. As soon as we prayed, in comes all of the doctors that cared for my mom for many years; her Kidney/Dialysis doctor, the doctors who helped with the healing of her feet, her regular doctor; all of them. I just found it so interesting and amazing that they took time out of their schedule to come and see her. As soon they left, I noticed a change in my mother's breathing; it had visibly gotten slower. I turned to my sister, and I told her, "She's going, mommas going." I just laid on her, and whispered in her ear, how much I appreciated her choosing me and loving me; how much I adored her and that I was going to miss her presence, but never forget the memories. I told her that I would see her again, and to tell dad hi for me. I watched her take her last breath, and instantly knew she was in the presence of the Lord. I knew that I was going to miss her tremendously, but I had peace that she was not in pain, and knowing that she was with her Lord was my comfort. I just looked at her for a moment; her spirit was gone, and what was left was now just a shell.

She was the best and closest example to me of a person who absolutely left this earth completely empty of the gifts and talents God gave her. In her emptying, she had some rough times and some great times. There was joy and tears. There was disappointment and excitement. She knew what it was like to have plenty, and to have nothing. In all of these seasons, she still loved; she still gave. Even in her last days, she was concerned about others, and if they had what they needed. She lost all of her material possessions, but the souls that were touched by her helping hand, her words of inspiration and love, her words that were not ashamed of the Gospel of Jesus Christ, which spoke more dynamically in her actions, are now the fruits and jewels of her crown in God's Kingdom.

When my adoptive mom passed in August of 2009, I found out why she avoided dealing with our sexual abuse. In talking with her sisters over lunch, I started to ask them about what she was like as an adolescent, because she only shared selective stories about her younger years. My Aunts told me that at age 17, my mom was sent away to Chicago by their mother to get her away from her father. She was being sexually abused by her father, and had attempted to kill her self twice. The second attempt, she tried to shoot herself.

As mothers, our first instinct is to nurture and protect our children. I will never fully know exactly how she felt, finding out that the children she so desperately wanted to love and care for were violated in the very way she was, and she could not protect us. It was easier for her to tuck her past deep down as far as it could go, than to talk about it. It was easier to just turn a blind eye, than to keep from having to dig up unresolved scars of her past. I believe she realized at the end of her time on this earth, that ignoring things of the past is not a highway towards peace. It's a sure way towards bondage, not just for you, but you can graft others into your bondage without even realizing it. Though she never verbally expressed her feelings about our abuse, I truly feel that she was sorry that it happened. Her response was only the result of what happened to her, and she never fully healed from it. I have come to learn this one thing, no one is perfect. We strive to do better, be better, and as we overcome, we can help someone else overcome.

I am a direct result of her faithfulness that obeyed God's call to act, and I now carry that same torch of passion, using the gifts and talents God has given me. She was a giant tree to me. The tree that showed a little girl how to view herself the way God viewed her…Redeemed. When I would hang my head low, she would tell me to look up; for all of my help comes from the Lord. It may have taken me a little longer to really receive this view, but in her death, everything that I have gone through and will go through, helps me to realize this.

Life is Testimony

~You never know ones story, until you've walked in their shoes...walk with me. ~

Genesis 5:22a
"And Enoch walked with God..."

As long as you get a hold of God's view of you, abide in His Word, and love people the way He loves you, you can't help but prosper. You will always have family. Not just blood family, birth family, but God's family; family that shares the same bloodline of Christ. For me, this family consists of a foster mother, an adoptive mother, aunts, friends, co-workers, business leaders, teachers, coaches, sisters, fathers, and grandmothers. We expect for God's view to line up with the most common sense ways, but I have learned that God never does anything ordinary to accomplish His extraordinary plan. He creatively draws us to

Him. At the beginning of my life, my view was extremely tunneled and closed, because of the things that I had endured. I was not completely connected to my lifeline in Christ, and in order for me to overcome; I had to do this, no matter how shameful or uncomfortable I felt.

Every day in my Christian walk, I have to choose to let go of thoughts or views that can delay all that God has for me. It's a process. We are to work out our own salvation in Christ. I had to let go of people's opinions and take the step that God was directing me to take, even when others didn't understand me or thought I was foolish. I refuse to die and take back to God the talents He has given me. No longer will fear, people's opinions, my past, or my circumstances be obstacles. I have some new challenges to face, but I will not allow negative baggage to hinder my growth and ability to move forward. If He can make a pathway in my wilderness to accomplish His Will, then surely, He can do that for you as well. Trust, patience, faith, Love, self-control, kindness, goodness, peace, joy, love, love, love...these have led me to *A View of Redemption*.

Closing

My view may not be your view, but redemption is for anyone and everyone to have. I would never have been able to overcome my past and all of the challenges I went through if it were not for my relationship with Christ. As I mentioned in the beginning of this book, this is the real reason why I shared my life in these pages with you. Something in my testimony connected to you. You may have never told anyone about your sexual abuse, or that you were a victim of rape, or conceived from rape. You may be on medication for depression or mental illness. You may go home and suffer from panic attacks. You may not know how to forgive those who have hurt you in some way. You may not have a God view of intimacy and how important it is to the marriage relationship. Your marriage might be on its last string. You may have been diagnosed with a horrible health report. You may not know how to manage your finances, or you may have secrets that you need to release and confess.

Everyone on the Earth, even atheists, knows that there is someone greater; that there is a Creator of all. Everyone is trying to find truth in some way. How we establish this truth has developed into a confusing mess of religion, tradition, folklore, and many other things. You can't look at this beautiful Earth and believe that a star blew up and created it. Your human spirit looks at creation and knows that there is a God. Every person who called themselves the Truth or the way to a better life is gone and back to the dust- dead. There is only One who lives, and His name is Jesus Christ. He sits right now at the right hand of God, eagerly waiting to come back for His church, His Bride; you, me, and many, many more. He is the Son of God. He died on a cross, shed his blood, defeated death and hell, and rose again, so that you may be free. No one was before Him, and there will never be another after Him.

By faith, I believe His Word, just like by faith you believe that if you sit in a chair, it's not going to break underneath of you. You probably don't even think about it breaking, you just know that it's going to hold you. There is truly only one way to deliverance. There is only one Truth, and one way to get to it. There is only one way to receive healing from abuse and all the things I've shared. The blood that Jesus shed was for you, so that you can now have relationship with your Creator God. It is through the blood of Christ that you are redeemed. Romans 10:9 says this, If we confess with our mouth, and believe in our hearts, that Jesus is Lord, and that God raised Him from the dead, we will be saved. We are all going to leave Earth one day, but leaving this Earth not knowing if you are going to heaven or hell is unsettling, don't you think? Eternity was present before we were even thought of, and it will be present after we leave. Why not walk a life of victory while you are here, and a life of victory in eternity? What do you have to lose?

If you want to begin the process of healing from brokenness, your opportunity is here. I admit that some change will not happen overnight; it didn't for me, but as my relationship grew in Christ, overcoming and deliverance just began to happen. As my soul prospered, I began to prosper. You will not be disappointed; you will be challenged, but you will learn to equip yourself with the Word of God to help you through these challenges...

You ready? Say this out loud:

God, I come to You in the Name of Jesus. I ask You to come into my life. I confess with my mouth that Jesus is my Lord and I believe in my heart that You have raised Him from the dead. I turn my back on sin and I commit to follow You for the rest of my life. I thank You, Father, for saving me!

Romans 10:9 (New King James Version)

"that if you confess with your mouth the Lord Jesus and believe in your heart that God has raised Him from the dead, you will be saved."

Congratulations,

You just began your road to Redemption. I have included in my book some additional resources I recommend to help you on your way. My senior Pastor, Dr. Wendy Treat of Christian Faith Center (Casey Treat Ministries), wrote a book called *Take a God*

Look at Yourself[6]. It is important for you to see God's view of you, and how to embrace and receive it.

The second book that I recommend is written by an amazing author, Deborah G. Hunter. Her book *The Call of Intercession*[7] speaks of prayer and how without developing a powerful prayer life, you truly will never know how to walk in relationship, direction, or the leading of God and His Spirit.

Who do you see when you look in the mirror? Someone you like? Or someone you like to pick apart? What most of us *don't* see is the TRUTH!

If you are like most people, you see yourself through eyes that are distorted. Your vision is clouded...possibly due to issues from your past, or just the negative things *you continually tell yourself about yourself*. We may "take a look at ourselves," but how many truly "take a God look" and see ourselves as He sees us?

Your self-image is how you *see* yourself and how you *feel* about yourself...it is the source of how you *act*—toward yourself and toward others.

Your self-image determines the success or failure of your relationships, your career, and your life. In short, it controls you and your behavior.

In this insightful book, Dr. Wendy Treat takes you on a journey into discovering the self-image God created and intended for you to have. Wendy's personal illustrations and sound Biblical teaching will show you how to identify the wrong image and exchange it for God's image of you.

Take a God look at yourself...see yourself through His eyes of love and acceptance...you'll never be the same!

Dr. Wendy Treat

Wendy pastors with her husband, Dr. Casey Treat, at Christian Faith Center, a church of 10,000 members with two locations in the Seattle, WA area. She and Casey have spent over 30 years building the local church and mentoring leaders around the world. Wendy's heart is for every Christian to grow in the knowledge of God's Word, enabling them to have victory in all areas of life.

For more information on Dr. Wendy Treat's ministry and products, visit wendytreat.com. Follow Wendy Treat on Facebook and Twitter. Her book is available at caseytreat.com and Amazon.com.

Take a God Look at Yourself
ISBN: 978-1-4499864-4-5
Paperback
$9.99

THE CALL OF
INTERCESSION

DEBORAH G. HUNTER

"Debbie Hunter is an extraordinary Christian woman who has made her life's assignment the pursuit of intercessory dimensions. As readers engage The Call of Intercession, they are taken on a journey into the private and holy chambers of the heart of this author who, by the aid of the Holy Spirit, is able to express the mind of God as it relates to this unique and significant assignment of prayer and intimacy with God."

~Dr. Keira Taylor-Banks
Executive Pastor
Living Waters Christian Fellowship
Newport News, Virginia

There is a clarion call going out to the Body of Christ to INTERCEDE for the nations of the world. We are seeing some of the worst economic, social & political times in our history unfold right before our very eyes. The Word of God tells us that we will know the time of His coming only by the signs that we see all around us. We have to begin now, if we have not already, to stand in the gap, take our position on the walls, and set up our posts in the towers. Will you answer the call?

Deborah G. Hunter

Deborah is owner & publisher of Hunter Heart Publishing. She and her husband Chris own several businesses aimed at supporting the Christian community through differing aspects of media outlets. They have launched STIR UP THE GIFT, which purposes to teach and train Christians how to seek God for the gift/gifts on the inside of them, as well as how to find the tools necessary to keep producing these gifts and how the recycling of these gifts will build the local Church and Church Body all over the world through missions and outreach.

Deborah G. Hunter is on Facebook, and you can follow Hunter Heart Publishing & Stir Up the Gift as well to find more of her resources. Her book is available at hunterheartpublishing.com, Amazon.com & BarnesandNoble.com.

The Call of Intercession
ISBN: 978-0-9823944-3-4
Paperback
$14.99

To contact Fahren J for book signings, speaking engagements, or to order bulk CD'S & Books, please e-mail publisher@hunterheartpublishing.com.

Check out official website at www.fahrenj.com and join her fan page on Facebook: FAHREN.

To book Fahren J for your next event, please contact Chris Hunter of Christ Hu Nterz Productions, LLC at kingdommusiq7@yahoo.com or ceo@christhunterzproductions.com, or call (757) 332-1962/ (253) 906-2160.

Notes

Chapter 9

[1] Casey Treat.: Renewing the Mind © 1999 Harrison House, Inc., Tulsa, Oklahoma.

[2] Christian Faith Center, A Casey Treat™ Ministry-P.O. Box 98800, Seattle, Washington 98198, www.caseytreat.com.

Chapter 11

[3] Abundant Life Ministries, Wapping Road, Bradford, West Yorkshire, BD3 0EQ, England, www.alm.org.uk.

[4] Pastor Charlotte Scanlon-Gambill: "What's In Your Cupboard?" Abundant Life Ministries- Bradford, West Yorkshire, England, www.alm.org.uk, www.charlottegambill.com.

Chapter 12

[5] Chomsky, Marvin J., Erman, John. (Directors). (1977). "Roots" [Motion Picture]. United States. David L. Wolper and Stan Margulies.

Closing

6 Wendy Treat: Take a God Look at Yourself © 2010 Casey Treat Ministries, Seattle, Washington.

7 Deborah G. Hunter: The Call of Intercession © 2010 Hunter Heart Publishing, DuPont, Washington.

Contact us:

Hunter Heart Publishing
P.O. Box 354
DuPont, Washington 98327

publisher@hunterheartpublishing.com

(253) 906-2160

www.hunterheartpublishing.com

"Offering God's Heart to a Dying World"